Martin J. Gössl
Great Queer Provocation

Queer Studies | Volume 43

Martin J. Gössl (Dr. phil.), born in 1983, is a professor of gender/queer studies at the Institute of Social Work at Fachhochschule Joanneum – Hochschule für Angewandte Wissenschaften in Graz (Austria). He is also the Women, Gender and Sexuality Network Representative of the Social Science and History Association (SSHA). His research interests include queer cultural and social dimensions in post-modern, virtualized societies.

Martin J. Gössl
Great Queer Provocation
The Seriously Playful Recognition Game

Translated from German by Henry Holland

[transcript]

Published with the support of the Austrian Science Fund (FWF): 10.55776/PUB1020

 Österreichischer Wissenschaftsfonds

Bibliographic information published by the Deutsche Nationalbibliothek
The Deutsche Nationalbibliothek lists this publication in the Deutsche Nationalbibliografie; detailed bibliographic data are available in the Internet at https://dnb.dnb.de/

This work is licensed under the Creative Commons Attribution 4.0 (BY) license, which means that the text may be remixed, transformed and built upon and be copied and redistributed in any medium or format even commercially, provided credit is given to the author.
https://creativecommons.org/licenses/by/4.0/
Creative Commons license terms for re-use do not apply to any content (such as graphs, figures, photos, excerpts, etc.) not original to the Open Access publication and further permission may be required from the rights holder. The obligation to research and clear permission lies solely with the party re-using the material.

First published in 2024 by transcript Verlag, Bielefeld
© Martin J. Gössl

Cover layout: Maria Arndt, Bielefeld
Cover illustration: Emil Srkalovic
Printed by: Majuskel Medienproduktion GmbH, Wetzlar
https://doi.org/10.14361/9783839473856
Print-ISBN: 978-3-8376-7385-2
PDF-ISBN: 978-3-8394-7385-6
ISSN of series: 2703-1365
eISSN of series: 2703-1373

Printed on permanent acid-free text paper.

For Manfreda: my unique furry companion.

Contents

1. Introduction 9
2. The Lead In 13
3. Queer Well-Being 23
4. Queer Success 37
5. Queer Diversions 53
6. Queer Sexuality 67
7. Queer Beauty 83
8. Queer Cultures 97
9. Queer Altercations 113
10. Queer Envy of Recognition 131

Bibliography 137

Index 149

1. Introduction

An engagement with queer theories that integrates real formulae for how people actually live together enriches us far beyond the bounds of applied science. Such an engagement is also essential for a spectrum of professions, social work and psychotherapy being but two of many. In everyday culture, experienced and represented realities of genders and sexualities are becoming more diverse, but also more relevant to the political conversation. The central argument here is not that aspects of gender and sexuality represent themselves more dominantly in public discourses today than in previous centuries. On the contrary, these aspects continue to be potentially volatile issues for societies, and thus continue to be subject to pressure from norms, legislation, labels, and stigmas. The guiding thought of these deliberations relates to the increasing replication of experience and representational forms, and of gender-based interpretations, within a framework of recognized possibilities—whether actors apprehend these choices legally, accept them, or merely tolerate them. There are, in short, more possibilities today than ever before.

When, decades ago, Queer Theory named the *disorder* emanating from heteronormativity by using a scholarly meta-concept, many theoretical treatises of that period drew inspiration from daily experience. This socio-cultural force was and is omnipresent in its tangibility, but so is the inestimable force of the resistance against this violence: defending taboos and deploying whataboutism are successful strategies until this day for undermining insights and critiques arising out of queer theory. An appropriate space for visibility means, on an utterly basic level, that at least some people recognize a specific issue, and with it a specific reality, which this recognition inaugurates as an element of human existence and/or of societal processes of interaction. In consequence, a discourse unfolds that's grounded in broad participation and informed by well-founded arguments and moral standpoints. Utilizing queer theory, and despite various forms of resistance, actors successfully established a broad discourse by the end of the last millennium, which featured political, academic, and cultural components. This development means it's now impossible to imagine away queerness as a lived reality.

For the current treatise, I consciously choose the applied perspective, and omit deliberately elaborate academic concepts in presenting forms of queer recognition as actual phenomena. The identification, presentation of, and analysis of the agendas identified all reflect this orientation toward concrete applications. That said, conceptional and theoretical impulses also complement this mix. Achieving a balance between the dimensions of application and the dimensions of theory is a welcome challenge in this process.

On the following pages, readers will encounter countless direct citations, which either supply concise impulses important for our theme, or serve as practical deliberations. Such excerpts are evidently always abridgments of the authors' further-reaching declarations. What's more, the excerpts drawn on here deliver clear statements, albeit an in abbreviated form, and deserve the space to replay some of their original impact. The challenge lies in how to embed these excerpts in the book's larger arguments. With that acknowledged, the standpoint presented in each case is intended to lead into discourse, or indeed provoke an alternative standpoint.

The refusal to lay claim comprehensiveness ought to be almost self-evident in the context of a queer publication. Neither the setting of agendas, nor the pointed emphases chosen, nor the references selected present a generalized picture. Instead, these can be read as fragments that have emerged as elementary in my own mind as author. No reader must concur with these without reservation, nor should readers necessarily identity with them. The focus selected, the argumentation strands, the interjections, or indeed the expressions chosen, are constantly a compromise at the expense of real, queer diversity. But the compromise is necessary and right, because this is the only way that a form of scholarship oriented toward applications can develop. This is the sole way to make possible queer realizations and debates, which are thrashed out in sub-cultural and intellectual milieus, but also in political milieus. In line with this aspiration, substantiated critiques are welcome, grounded refutations are actively desired, and alternative interpretations are considered motivational.

One of the hardest conceptual lines to draw surely relates to the question of whether mental space for the verbalization of thoughts should be adduced as an example of the cognitive challenges faced here. Or to put it differently: where should we draw the boundaries in this exposition, which at least seems to be a global one? The definition of postmodern and virtually interconnected societies is an assisting construct, with which to detach oneself, genuinely, from geographical spaces, and with which to understand queerness as a socio-cultural phenomenon, which has been able to surface because of historical occurrences and virtual interconnections. It is precisely the multifariousness and openness of a queer approach that makes a setting of boundaries on a geographical or even social basis impossible. Queer realities are able to take in both virtual and real performances and spaces, conventions and trends, knowledge and truths, and much, much more, without being bound to a single location, person, or form of interpretation.

Many of the thoughts presented here have arisen from discussions and everyday altercations, scholarly and scientific studies, and theoretical immersions. All these animating and inspiring moments have helped shape the final book. Moreover, the questions of why this publication has been undertaken, and how its points of departure have been selected, are above all questions of personal standpoint, albeit accompanied by a necessary positioning in the scholarly-scientific landscape. Particularly in recent years, I've had new and more profound possibilities of participating in both a European and North American discourse sphere. In my scholarship and in my private life, the liveliness of New York and Graz in Austria genuinely make them spaces that influence my reflections. At the same time, I'm conscious that an individual life also always means geographical, social, and cultural limitations.

2. The Lead In

> When they ushered us out, they very nicely put you out the door. Then you're standing across the street in Sheridan Square Park. But why? Everybody's looking at each other. ... Suddenly, the nickels, dimes, pennies, and quarters started flying. I threw quarters, and pennies, and whatnot. ... To be there was so beautiful. It was so exciting.[1]

With these words, the activist Sylvia Rivera described her personal impressions of the Stonewall Revolution of 1969 in New York City. In an interview given in 1998, just four years before her death, she provided a more precise account of what had happened:

> I was a radical, a revolutionist. I am still a revolutionist. ... I'm glad I was in the Stonewall Riot. I remember when someone threw a Molotov cocktail, I thought, "My god, the revolution is here. The revolution is finally here!" I always believed that we would have a fightback. I just knew that we would fight back. I just didn't know it would be that night. I am proud of myself as being there that night. If I had lost that moment, I would have been kinda hurt because that's when I saw the world change for my people and me.[2]

---

1   Eric Marcus, *Making Gay History, The Half-Century Fight for Lesbian and Gay Equal Rights* (New York: Harper Perennial, 2002), 138n.
2   Leslie Feinberg, "Youth of color form STAR – Street Transvestite Action Revolutionaries, Lavender & red, part 73," article from 1970, cited in: *Workers World*, September 24, 2006, www.workers.org and in *Workers World*, March, 2021: https://workers.org/2006/us/lavender-red-73/.

Until her death, Sylvia Rivera was unquestionably a critical and nonconformist activist in the US LGBTIQ movement.[3] Her experiences as a drag queen—the category through which she self-identified—on New York's streets in the early 1960s certainly left their mark. Harassment and physical assaults from the police, and indeed, from almost anyone else, were the order of the day. The utter lack of respect in police custody has been described by other protagonists in equally bad or even worse terms: the danger of being raped during a prison sentence constituting just one form of thoroughly abusive treatment.[4]

An eyewitness of events, Rivera described the decisive night in late June 1969 as warm and close. The police first entered the bar, and then turned off the music. After that, those who had been socializing in the bar were led outside, then cooped up between a fence and police vehicles. Then suddenly things kicked off: coins were flying through the air, soon followed by bottles:[5]

> We were not taking any more of this shit. We had done so much for other movements. It was time. It was street gay people from the Village out front: homeless people who lived in the park in Sheridan Square outside the bar-and then drag queens behind them and everybody behind us.[6]

After her death in February 2002, Riki Wilchins' obituary introduced Sylvia Rivera with the following words:

> She may have been the prototypical Angry Queen. Unbowed, unbought, and virtually indigestible by a gay movement she helped birth, Stonewall warrior Sylvia Rivera died on February 19 of end-

---

3 LGBTIQ = lesbian, gay, bisexual, trans, inter, queer people.
4 Ehn Nothing, *Street Transvestite Action Revolutionaries: Survival, Revolt, and Queer Antagonist Struggle* (New York: Untorelli Press 2013), available as PDF: https://untorellipress.noblogs.org/files/2011/12/STAR.pdf, 12.
5 Nothing, *Street*, 12.
6 Nothing, *Street*.

stage liver disease aggravated by too many years on alcohol and city streets.[7]

Critically, and entirely in the spirit of the woman who died, Wilchin noted:

> In 2002, butches, queens, fairies, high femmes, drag people, tomboys, and sissies have all but vanished from official gay discourse. They are rarely mentioned in the public pronouncements of major gay organizations. Federal gay rights legislation pending in Congress doesn't mention gender expression or identity, nor does the gay rights bill pending in Albany. In effect, gender has become the new 'gay,' the thing you don't talk about in polite or political company.[8]

Sylvia Rivera fought a long and exhausting struggle to have her issues—and at times even her own person—recognized. Both within and beyond a queer community, Rivera often had a hard time of it, even decades after the occurrences centered on the Stonewall Inn. She wanted people to take notice of her as an activist, and to be recognized as a human being from a specific community. In one scene captured in Randy Wicker's documentary footage, this becomes all too evident: even when homeless, and in her temporary shelter on the pier of Manhattan's meatpacking district, Rivera squares up to difficult questions.[9] Despite her catastrophic living conditions, Rivera's enthusiasm is tangible, as is her passion for her own activist narrative. She casts herself as perhaps *the* elementary figure in a queer movement, which developed from the fires at the Stonewall Inn in 1969 to become an efficacious force in its own right. Amidst all of life's impasses, her version of the story appears to have become more important than life itself for Rivera. Moreover, it's made to function as an explicative formula for a lived past, and for a present that still must be overcome.

---

7   Riki Wilchins, "A Women for Her Time," in *The Village Voice*, February 26, 2002.
8   Wilchins, "Women."
9   "Randy Wicker interviews Sylvia Rivera on the Pier," viewed at Vimeo.com, https://vimeo.com/37548074.

But Rivera's own biographical narrative took a tragic turn, when leading historians had no choice but to confirm there were discrepancies in the accounts she had given of events. Graver still, evidence accumulated that Rivera hadn't even been present on the day of the events in and around the Stonewall Inn. David Carter, the renowned author and expert on the Gay Revolution of 1969, has spent years painstakingly researching the incidents of that period, and recording them in his book on the subject in minute detail. In his article on the fiftieth anniversary of Stonewall, he arrives at the following conclusion:

> The evidence, when looked at as a whole, suggests that Rivera was not at the Uprising [i.e. the Stonewall Revolution] but became involved with GAA [Gay Activist Alliances – a queer organization in that period] in early 1970, as the beginning of a long career of activism. Over time, as she came to appreciate how celebrated an event Stonewall was and how much credit her friend Marsha P. Johnson [an equally well-known female activist in the revolution] received for setting everything off, Rivera began to say that she too had been there, tying her account to the already existing narrative about Johnson, who had woken her up on the first night of the Uprising to tell her about it.[10]

Based on the facts before him, David Carter, who died in 2020, raised valid doubts about Rivera's personal narratives of events, through working together with the historian Martin Duberman. Rivera's statements were contradictory, and, what's more, it was possible to prove after the event that Rivera herself had attempted to be incorporated into factual histories of the Revolution.[11] It was unbelievably important for her to gain assurance that her personal narratives had been recognized as part of queer history in general. At the very least, she wanted to know that she, as an individual human, had been added to the revolutionary experience.

---

10   Cited in: David Carter, "Exploding the Myths of Stonewall," in: *gcn* [Gay City News], June 27, 2019, https://www.gaycitynews.com/exploding-the-myths-of-stonewall/.
11   David Carter, "Exploding."

Sylvia Rivera's achievements were exceptional. Her role as a groundbreaking fighter for queer recognition is incontestable. These achievements remain, even though, after initial successes, marginalized groups were too rapidly forced back to the edges of society, and into renewed societal invisibility. Her life was shaped by deep psychological lows, but also by rebellion. Her urge for the kind of recognition that people took seriously was all too understandable, as was her desire to become visible, along with her issues. This was what had connected her to others, and to herself. Moreover, Rivera is exemplary for how forms of recognition in a queer community have great difficulty expressing themselves. Her whole life long, Rivera was torn between her wish for a broader and more valued sort of visibility, and the resistance displayed against queer abbreviations. The processes by which certain queer subcultures became invisible made her furious, but motivated her concurrently to kick back against such pressures. The ways in which her person was perceived were no less ambivalent: she met with a great lack of understanding, but also, at times, with respect. Rivera built up her own mental memorial—often through actions that drew much attention, but which she didn't always consider so important—and knocked it down at the same time, by searching for specific forms of recognition. While many of her stories and reports should be treated with caution from today's perspective, especially considering the historical research that's now available, the queer postmortem cult of Rivera the activist is more lively and visible than ever. It would have been a great joy if she could have experienced it.

Are we talking here about one's own story as an act of political revolution, or merely about a spontaneous, coincidental revolt of frustrated party guests? About practices of showing esteem for queer variety and complexity, or just about same-sex desire and various gender-based imitations? Sylvia Rivera is only one example in a multitude of better-known and less well-known human destinies, who, in the course of their lives, have experienced many recognizing but also disqualifying structures, imposed by both queer and non-queer communities. To be more precise: subcultural communities—like societies in general—produce forms of communicating esteem and visibility, which feed into a concept of visibility. This concept can be similar to, or in line with, a general societal majority, but it's just as possible that it displays differences or specialties.

These introductory insights should fuel curiosity, in both its historical mantle, and in its social and cultural anthropology guise, to uncover more of substance about forms of autonomous and heteronomous recognition in a queer community, operating in a queer community located in a world of economic well-being.

The question of exclusion within the queer community remains on the agenda even now, midway through the twenty-first century. Grindr, for example, the largest dating platform for gay men, has set up the initiative "Kindr Grindr"[12] to combat accusations of racism that have been brought against it:

> Dating and hook-up service Grindr has announced its intention to remove the "ethnicity filter" from its popular app. The controversial function allowed paying users to filter out prospective partners based on ethnicity labels such as "Asian," "Black," and "Latino." Long criticized as racist, the filter also helped to create a culture where users were emboldened to express their racism. ... Alongside other dating apps, Grindr has a reputation for sexual racism – the exclusion of potential partners based on race. In 2017, Grindr tried to amend this perception with the "Kindr Grindr" initiative. This move banned the use of exclusionary language such as "No Asians" and "No Blacks" in user bios, and attempted to explain to users why these statements are harmful and unacceptable.[13]

This demonstrates, to pursue one line of argument, that this platform's users are offered the opportunity of inserting themselves into ethnic categories. Concurrently, it evidently has been and continues to be possible

---

12   See: "Kindr Grindr," https://www.kindr.grindr.com/.
13   Gene Lim, Brady Robards, and Bronwyn Carlson, "Grindr is deleting its 'ethnicity filter.' But racism is still rife in online dating," *Conversation*, June 7, 2020, https://theconversation.com/grindr-is-deleting-its-ethnicityfilter-but-racism-is-still-rife-in-online-dating-140077.

for certain member groups to apply these same categories in the partner search function. In itself, this is neither basis nor cause for existing processes of recognition being how they are. But it is still a clear manifestation of the same:

> Overall, researchers have found that racialized language and interaction is pervasive in online partner-seeking venues catering to gay/bisexual men and that gay/bisexual men of color are regularly exposed to such language and interactions. Based on the literature, researchers have indicated that both rejection on the basis of race and objectification on the basis of race are frequently encountered by gay/bisexual men of color in a sexualized context. Moreover, researchers have described some facets of RSD [Racialized Sexual Discrimination] that are unique to online settings, such as user profiles that display exclusionary (e.g. "no Blacks") or inclusionary (e.g. "Whites only") race-based preferences. Finally, researchers have described instances in which outright hostile and degrading comments directed toward racial/ethnic minorities are communicated in these online settings. Thus, these four categories (rejection, objectification, exclusionary/inclusionary preferences, and degradation) may capture a broad scope of how RSD is experienced and enacted online.[14]

Well-founded research has demonstrated that the consequences of such behavior are far reaching, for the everyday culture of a queer community, and for the individuals affected. Particular ethnic codes, which can be "read" by looking at images of a person's appearance, determine in both virtual and analogue processes the outcome of interactions—whether and in which form recognition will be expressed:

> The desirability of white men was not limited to other white men. Instead, gay men of color indicated that white men were also preferred by men of color as well. More than simply a preference for white men,

---

14 Ryan Wade and Gary Harper, "Racialized Sexual Discrimination (RSD) in the Age of Online Sexual Networking: Are Young Black Gay/Bisexual Men (YBGBM) at Elevated Risk for Adverse Psychological Health?" *American Journal of Community Psychology* 65, no. 3–4 (2019): 14. https://doi.org/10.1002/ajcp.12401.

there was also active exclusion of men of color by white men and by other men of color. When white men did prefer men of color as sexual partners over other white men, gay men of color understood that their desirability was based on largely stereotypical traits associated with their race. For example, Black men were favored for being sexually aggressive and possessing large penises while Asian men were favored for being sexually submissive. ... More damaging was the impact that sexual racism had on the self-esteem of gay men of color. Gay men of color often felt marginalized and frustrated in the larger gay community as a result of their sexual exclusion. Thus, sexual racism had both a sexual and social consequence for gay men of color.[15]

Both case studies selected here—Sylvia Rivera's historicized performance and racism in virtual dating racism—reveal the tough struggles that continue to surround queer recognition. That said, it's primarily those affected who are in a position to articulate a critique grounded in societal politics, or indeed a scholarly and scientific critique. Yet demands voiced by those affected for efforts towards inclusion appear to go unheeded, the same fate that has befallen similar demands that the queer community have raised against majorities in society. The strategy of exclusion, which so many people have lived experience of, thus reproduces itself unreflectively, and is merely milled down into finer granules, and tailored to meet the needs of subgroups inside a particular subculture. Whiteness, hegemonic masculinity, and ableism are only three of many social influencing factors that affect human individuals.

Assuming we can ascertain the forms of autonomous and heteronomous recognition of a queer community, in a virtually interconnected world that's currently in a state of economic well-being: which consistencies, or indeed disjunctions, can we identify in today's world?

Responding to this structuring question, attention shall be devoted to six life areas in the chapters that follow, which contain hidden within

---

15 Han Chong-suk and Choi Kyung-Hee, "Very Few People Say 'No Whites': Gay Men of Color and The Racial Politics of Desire," *Sociological Spectrum* 38, no. 3, (2018): 18n, https://doi.org/10.1080/027 32173.2018.1469444.

them forms of recognizing, but also disqualifying, the lending of prestige: *wealth, success, entertainment, sexuality, beauty, and culture.* These dimensions can exemplify the continuity and adaptability that influential mechanisms have on queer everyday culture. This exact observation reveals not just sociocultural capriciousness, but also, and to the same extent, the widespread readiness of both queer and non-queer people to collaborate—in full consciousness that those who don't follow the stipulations will have to bear the consequences. The same applies for queer escalations, which again, and in a more profound fashion, expose overarching dynamics. The following pages are intended to provide an argumentative terrain in which all these ideas and issues can be given full rein, in order to initialize analysis and reflection. The goal, in so doing, is in no way to articulate a solution but rather to lay bare an existing discourse, and to carry it into the future.

3. Queer Well-Being

One of the most tenacious myths clinging to a specifically gay subculture is the conjecture that soi-disant pink dollars are going to continue growing on trees forever. For decades, a piece of misinformed capitalist gossip has prevailed, claiming that the facts of a general absence of kids, and couples consisting of two men, is going to leave a clear economic footprint—on the healthy state of people's bank balances. This turns belief in economic well-being into a chimera, not only of ascription, but also of self-attribution. What we deduce from this underscores the following insight:

> Luxury consumption is the mean by which gay male consumers identity themselves as group members, and therefore by their consumption they reinforce the fact that their identity and self-concept are shaped by the norms of the group. For that reason, group members associate themselves with the brands that their group consume, and have a connection with these specific brands in order to form the self that has the similar traits, preferences and qualities. The gay subculture can have a direct and strong impact on the individuals' brand attitude and choices. The greater the brand serves as a sort of an identification, the greater that gay male consumers [sic] as individuals are willing to consumer luxury brands.[1]

---

[1] Hiba Dib and Lester W Johnson, "Gay Male Consumers Seeking Identity in Luxury Consumption: The Self-Concept," *International Journal of Business Marketing and Management (IJBMM)* 4, no. 2 (2019): 33.

This research reinforces the notion that gay men tend to purchase luxury goods as symbols of identity and status. The purchasing of consumer goods shapes one's own performance, i.e. how a personality represents themselves to the outside world, although it must be added that the plethora of goods available facilitates qualitative differences and individual standpoints. But is this enough to prove the pink dollar phenomenon exists?

For years, attempts have regularly been undertaken to throw light on the real economic situations of queer people groups. One meta-analysis conducted by the School of Law at the University of California, Los Angeles (UCLA), encompassing the whole of the USA, came to following conclusions: the income of heterosexual men came in above salary payments to gay colleagues carrying out the same professional activities. A higher percentage of trans people are unemployed than in the population as a whole, and those in paid employment have low average incomes. In general, gay, lesbian, bisexual, and trans-identifying people routinely continue to file complaints about discrimination in the workplace based on their gender or sexual identity.[2]

When this analysis is put side by side with current data from 2019 from the same institute, then we can conclude that nine percent of LGBT people in the USA were affected by unemployment, but only five percent of non-LGBT people. Moreover, twenty-five percent of LGBT people had to get by on an annual income of under $ 25,000, whereas the same fate befell only eighteen percent of non-LGBT people.[3] When we go into more detail, we see that:

> Gay and straight cisgender men at first appear to have similarly low (when compared to women) poverty rates, and bisexual cisgender men and transgender people have higher poverty rates than cisgender straight men. After accounting for differences in race, age, education,

---

[2] See: M.V. Lee Badgett, Holning Lau, Brad Sears, and Deborah Ho, *Bias in the Workplace: Consistent Evidence of Sexual Orientation and Gender Identity Discrimination* (Los Angeles: UCLA, The Williams Institute, 2007), https://escholarship.org/uc/item/5h3731xr.

[3] See: Badgett et al., 4.

and other relevant characteristics, gay men are indeed just as likely to be poor as cisgender straight men. In addition, the higher rates of poverty initially seen for bisexual men disappeared after accounting for their different characteristics compared to cisgender straight men. We find that transgender people consistently have the highest odds of being poor among all groups, even after accounting for their characteristics. Where people live matters for poverty rates. In particular, LGBT people are less likely to live in rural areas compared to cisgender straight people, but LGBT people living in rural areas have particularly high rates of poverty.[4]

It's possible to consolidate this picture by zooming in with the scholarly microscope onto specific subcategories:

> In most states, LGBT women have insufficient legal protections if they are fired or denied housing simply because of who they are or who they love. Additionally, when two women build a life together, they amplify the wage gap between men and women, resulting in lower income and higher rates of poverty. Transgender women, LGBT women of color, LGBT women raising children, and older LGBT women are especially vulnerable. Lack of legal recognition of LGBT women's families can mean higher taxes, lower retirement benefits, denial of family health insurance, inability to take family medical leave and more.[5]

On this evidence, the widely established narrative of a specifically queer variety of economic well-being does not stand scrutiny: the complete opposite is true for numerous queer, subcultural domains. The economic ascendancy of a white, heteronormative form of masculinity stands unbowed. The attraction some gay men feel toward luxury goods represents

---

4   M. Badgett, S. Choi, and B.D. Wilson, B. D., *LGBT Poverty in the United States: A study of differences between sexual orientation and gender identity groups* (Los Angeles: Williams Institute, 2019), 27, https://escholarship.org/uc/item/37b617z8.

5   Movement Advancement Project and Center for American Progress, *Paying an unfair Price: The Financial Penalty for LGBT Women in America* (Denver: Center for American Progress, 2015), 44. https://www.icrw.org/wp-content/uploads/2016/11/paying-an-unfair-price-lgbt-women.pdf.

an attempt at cultural appropriation, aimed at communicating images of well-being, within one's own circles and to the outside. In this process, economic well-being is transformed into a measurable unit, with which social valence can be obtained in interpersonal interaction—albeit only if the criterion in question is recognized. But this transformation distorts the concept of well-being, detaching it from its primary meaning:

> Economic well-being is defined as having present and future financial security. Present financial security includes the ability of individuals, families, and communities to consistently meet their basic needs (including food, housing, utilities, health care, transportation, education, child care, clothing, and paid taxes), and have control over their day-to-day finances. It also includes the ability to make economic choices and feel a sense of security, satisfaction, and personal fulfillment with one's personal finances and employment pursuits. Future financial security includes the ability to absorb financial shocks, meet financial goals, build financial assets, and maintain adequate income throughout the life-span.
> Economic well-being may be achieved by individuals, families, and communities through public policies that ensure the ability to build financial knowledge and skills, access to safe and affordable financial products and economic resources, and opportunities for generating income and asset-building. It occurs within a context of economic justice within which labor markets provide opportunities for secure full-employment with adequate compensation and benefits for all.[6]

It appears that queer interpretations of (economic) well-being prevailing in some places cannot be compared directly to the statistics of how the situation actually is, or to a pre-defined standard. But building a bridge to the queer past can offer some explanations:

> I have argued that lesbian and gay identity and communities are historically created, the result of process of capitalistic development

---

6   Council on Social Work Education, Working Definition of Economic Well-Being, https://www.cswe.org/Centers-Initiatives/Initiatives/Clearinghouse-for-Economic-Well-Being/Working-Definition-of-Economic-Well-Being.

that has spanned many generations. A corollary of this argument is that we are not a fixed social minority composed for all time of a certain percentage of the population. There are more of us than one hundred years ago, more of us than forty years ago. And there may very well be more gay men and lesbians in the future. Claims made by gays and nongays that sexual orientation is fixed at an early age, that large numbers of visible gay men and lesbians in society, the media, and the schools will have no influence in sexual identities of the young, are wrong. Capitalism has created the material conditions for homosexuals' desire to express itself as a central component of some individuals' lives; now, our political movements are changing consciousness, creating the ideological conditions that make it easier for people to make that choices. ... In this respect gay men and lesbians are well situated to play a special role. Already excluded from families as most of us are, we have had to create, for our survival, networks of support that do not depend on the bonds of blood or the license of a state, but that are freely chosen and nurtured.[7]

The historian John D'Emilios argues that forms of social relations out with traditional family-type constructs are a necessary alternative in order to survive socially, at least for some participants in the queer community.

An individual's economic autonomy functions as both existential foundation and base for the creation of free zones—free in interpersonal, cultural, and other senses of the word. This facilitation of sketches for one's own life encompasses particularly those personal spheres, which have previously been made taboo, or have been highly restricted at the very least, because of traditional, spiritual, or milieu-specific circumstances. It is hardly a surprise to reaffirm that this kind of autonomy makes it possible for individuals to dodge the rigid net of expectations, pertaining to particular social environments, which have often applied pressure to choices about gender, sexuality, and

---

7   John D'Emilio, "Capitalism and Gay Identity," in: Henry Abelove, Michele Aina Barale and David M. Halperin, *The Lesbian and Gay Studies Reader* (New York: Routledge, 1993), 473ff.

relationship forms. This autonomy shoves this array of duties to the side, or even rejects them explicitly and entirely, in order to experience and enact a same-gender orientation, or to construct an unconventional lifestyle. The phenomena of financial well-being is able to break open the economic autonomy of conventional and compartmentalized social systems—including a family—but in no way releases the individual from the wish to be part of a community. The stride into the queer world can be motivated by desire, but also by the wish to be part of a community. This self-determined appropriation of a collective identity—of a queer community, for example—must be understood as part of an undeniable chain of actions, undertaken to evade being the threat of human isolation. Even when family-based organizations continue to exist into the twenty-first century—or are even reconstructed, for example in the form of LGBTIQ families—the lived, social model of queer individuality resists, nonetheless, dominant understandings of societal majorities. Or to express the matter differently: how many people are already lucky enough to be born into a queer family? The divergence between an individual's inbred habitat and the habitat that individual desires remains tangible, experiential, and visible, which is why move community alternatives, in all their manifold forms, are carried out.

That said, nobody, and no community, can create value-free spaces, emptied of all norms, clichés, and attributions. Every collective develops in its gatherings and group dynamic processes values and attitudes that seem appropriate to it: these shift over time, and occasionally seem to be arbitrary. What's more: many such norms are applied unreflectively, and yet establish themselves as subcultural standards. In this manner, the pink dollars myth has somehow got stuck inside queer communities' self-perceptions, and in how those out with the community perceive queer participants. The pink dollars myth is kept alive as both an ideal and as an attribution.

The causes of this complementary dynamic lie in aspirations towards personal satisfaction and recognition. Explicative approaches that go deeper are required to respond to the question of why queer (economic) well-being wants to experience itself prestigiously, in the form of luxury articles.

In raising this question, it's right to point out that investigations into satisfaction versus prosperity relations are hardly new. Many transnational unions, alliances, and associations gather data about income development within states, parallel to figures concerning the population's satisfaction. When these quantitative elicitations are combined with qualitative questionnaires, it becomes possible for those interpreting to draw conclusions. As is the case in the following analysis on the European Union's member states:

> Furthermore, it has been demonstrated that household income levels among those questionees is less important, regarding their satisfaction with their own financial situation, than the standard of living realized within their household structure. Consequently, one could assume that improved material living circumstances within the EU would result in satisfaction levels corresponding with the financial situation [at individual household level].[8]

Consequently, the convergence of material living conditions is a primary aspect in how individuals experience their own satisfaction. This convergence can match with an average value for society as a whole, or orient itself toward a subculturally defined ideal, in the form of a perceived or estimated median. We thus have options to select from to define lines of reference for an experienced prosperity, whereby, again, the social-cultural location makes its impact. To simplify: do the self-imposed reference values focus on statistical averages for the whole population, or on the queer community, or even exclusively on upper income sections in society? Dependent on whether the comparison is used in one's own interpretation of prosperity and satisfaction, the clearer the difference that manifests itself, in both positive and negative terms. Convergence towards an economic norm, and a norm of recognition, is subordinate to individual and subcultural parameters, which

---

8   Christoph Bernhard, "Wohlstand wichtiger als Einkommen für Zufriedenheit mit der finanziellen Situation: Untersuchungen zur Zufriedenheit mit der finanziellen Situation im europäischen Vergleich," *Informationsdienst Soziale Indikatoren (ISI)*, no. 26 (2001): 15, https://doi.org/10.15464/isi.26.2001.12-15.

do not have to be constructed exclusively according to the formats of a queer community. Instead, these can also reflect other dimensions of constructing references—including vocational training, nationality, or profession. Moreover, and depending on the situation, further lines of reference can be maintained. These include recognizing several subcultures, and/or the majority-based society with which subcultures seek psychological interaction. These individual referential values are transformable and changeable, and in no way rigidly fixed—although constant and internalized parameters, including minimum standards, can emerge.

It's precisely understandings of economic well-being that are co-determined by a range of social and cultural influences, and that are shaped by regional and milieu-specific factors. Codes that are able to express prosperity must be "written" in such a way that large numbers of observers can actually understand them as codes. The point of reference in question needs the immediate environment to identify it as such, so that it can then be refashioned as a form of recognition:

> The thesis defended here argues that the question of "prosperity" and a new kind of "progress" at the end of the neoliberal era, in all these and other arenas [discussed previously], is not purely a question of definition, which can be reduced down to an unbiased prioritization and balancing out of macroeconomic indicators. On the contrary, this is a question of power. Whoever triumphs in the debate on the question of how economic growth, prosperity, and progress should be defined and measured, wins concurrently interpretive sovereignty over which development paths, in the sense of both societal politics and national economics, should be pushed for, and which neglected.[9]

---

9   Matthias Ecke and Sebastian Petzold, "Die Vermessung des Fortschritts, Konkurrierende Strategien zur Verallgemeinerung widerstreitender Wachstumsverständnisse," in: *Wohlstand, Wachstum, Investitionen, Junge Wissenschaft für wirtschaftlichen und sozialen Fortschritt*, ed. René Bormann et al. (Bonn: Friedrich-Ebert-Stiftung, 2012), 10n.

A socioeconomic perspective, as outlined here by Ecke and Petzold, relates prosperity to growth and progress. Such a method of looking at society as a whole can encompass macroeconomic dimensions anchored in neoliberal structures, although any extended perspective increasingly brings questions of power up to the surface, power questions that then seem more decisive for prosperity outcomes on personal and subcultural levels. Broad swathes of the population enjoying prosperity connect strongly to power mechanisms for redistributing wealth, and to the socio-political patronage of economic development opportunities. The collective invents and applies possibilities for distributing wealth—these can range from effective, to social, to rather limited and minimalist. Moreover, social networks in politics, culture, and above all the economy impact through personal alliances (based on favoritism) and favor, or even facilitate in the first place, individual economic successes. Both forms of prosperity, the collective and the individual, are subordinate in these processes to powerful everyday cultures, in which norms, standards, and ethics function as implicit, or sometimes even explicit, criteria of belonging. To concretize these criteria, gender, sexual orientation, skin color and many more factors are applied. This is a granting of status to specific forms of power, which, even when these are not comprehensible, at least must be recognized by the majority. This recognition of a powerful prosperity makes intense, playful usage of the myth of attainability. Additionally, it provides symbolic identifications. Some of these identifications can be acquired, and also facilitate detailed differentiations.

Although mechanisms of exclusion and inclusion result from these implications, it's possible to combat these, at least up to a certain point.

Along the paths described, the action interface of queer thinking on prosperity finds itself on the same normative playing field as other sub-communities. Engaging on this field leads inevitably to the emergence of forms of community-based recognition—or disdain—and to the creation of subcultural elites. Are then all subcultural communities subject to the same principle and in the same intensity, or are some really queerer? The dominant and neoliberal triangulation of prosperity, growth, and progress, in the sense of John D'Emilio's historical treatment of the subject, is possibly anchored more profoundly in a specifically queer concept of prosperity. This becomes clearer when we consider the following exposition:

Personal growth toward autonomy, but also toward economic independence, requires a community development that can provide the individual with space and structures. Consequently, the will to work must be combined with the factual possibility of paid employment. Leaving the family unit, or even risking breaking with your family completely because of a queer identity, necessitates the existence of socioeconomic options and perspectives, particularly when the freely-chosen queer identity should be expressed in a publicly visible way, or at least not hidden. Such a change fuels the urge toward the individual freedom offered by individual economic growth, and with that, in a further step, the concurrent economic growth—seen from an overarching perspective—of a queer subculture. Of course, there have always been individuals who, despite hostile conditions in the politics of a given society, have been able to initiate an appropriate individualization: Oscar Wilde for example,[10] whose family and economic background was in no way average for his period. Yet it's precisely these individual examples that demonstrate that acquiring personal and subcultural prosperity must be understood as a socioeconomic law, utterly necessary for the formation of a visible and broad-based queerness. This strong connection between understanding prosperity and understanding personal growth has a special significance from a queer perspective: the imperative has been and continues to apply this connection. Queerness impacts people individually and independently from social, family, cultural, economic, national, or other factors.

The idea of progress, which manifests itself just as dominantly in a queer subculture, seems harder to pinpoint, but the following contribution helps us to do so:

> This ethical life, as an alternating form of the recognition of personal differences based on a shared understanding, of legal systems or of values, forms the identification foundation for the development of

---

10   Matthew Sturgis, *Oscar: A Life*, (London: Apollo, 2018).

community-based solidarity. According to Honneth,[11] the formation of this solidarity depends on the degree of pluralization occurring in a socially defined value horizon, on the character of personality ideals recorded in the same, on the unbowed power of religious or metaphysical traditions, and on cultural forms of self-understanding. Regarding pluralistic society, Honneth identifies ... a starting point for solidarity in the fact that subjects can obtain social recognition along the path of individual achievements appropriate to own self-realizations. Or put differently, each individual having the opportunity to achieve standing is a value that has established itself in pluralistic society. In practice however, the normative insight, that each of our fellow humans must have the chance to achieve social status, must be fought for time after time for specific but also changing groups of society's members. When a number of minorities, including, for example, the majority of immigrants—who live long-term with an inferior legal status—do not experience sufficient vindication, or even sufficient forms of integration based on them being valued socially, this can limit long-term the identification of these later, potential citizens with the population as a whole.[12]

Evidently, this explanation based on inferior legal status can be transferred onto the queer community's long history, which is why acquiring social status in this context—progress in the recognition of a particular majority-based perception of others—is of central importance. The progress referred to in this case applies primarily to a societal politics dimension that is constantly affecting the individual and their possibilities. In further consequence, this progress also encompasses sociocultural dimensions that manifest themselves in interpersonal forms of interaction. The recognition of queer individuals in specific milieus has happened, and continues to happen, far from the plane of legal equality

---

11   See: Axel Honneth, *Das Recht der Freiheit, Grundriss einer demokratischen Sittlichkeit*, (Frankfurt: Suhrkamp, 2011).
12   Anita Horn, "Anerkennung und Freiheit, Subjekttheoretische Grundlagen einer Theorie demokratischer Sittlichkeit," *Archiv für Rechts- und Sozialphilosophie (ARSP)* 104 (2018): 38n. Last accessed March, 2021: https://doi.org/10.5167/uzh-123911.

of opportunity, which is why both dimensions of this kind of progress are relevant. However, it's also possible that milieu-specific disadvantages continue to exist, and to exert a strong influence, even when legal equality for highly varied areas of queer life has been achieved.

Growth and progress are inherent components of a prosperity concept for queer communities. In many of their facets, they go beyond a single "moment" experienced through a whole society. Moving closer to the norm in the guise of prosperity has been a process which, for many subcultural, peripheral groups in the past, has proven itself a reliable vehicle. Concurrently, this image of prosperity must also be understand as a form of potential queer inversion. Recognizable areas for performance are provided for by conforming to social and cultural parameters that shape the whole of society, and by showing off symbols of prosperity.[13] This is as true for a general community as for a subcultural one.

This aspiration is motivated by the wish to move closer to the norm *and* the notion of an exclusive separation from members of one's own group. The idea is that the stigmatized kind of Being-Other ought to be reduced, while a form of self-representation that seems exclusive is reproduced. In so doing, the present realities of the queer economic situation, which have been researched regularly for years, is shoved into the background, enabling the pink dollars myth to live on, indomitable. If we now add to this dynamic the media image of the queer community, this chimera built out of wish and attribution appears perfect:

> If middle-class propriety is a condition of good queerness, how does the representational field of popular culture make room for worthy, sexual queers from nonprofessional and working-class circumstances? The answer is "infrequently" ... That is a draining conclusion, however, if it means that queer class life has nowhere to go and nothing to do except to live with the limits dominance imposes, learning class rules from the cultural ether, and infusing that air with resignation in turn. What, alternately, might solidarity look and feel like? If it is true that

---

13   Judith Butler, "Imitation and Gender Insubordination" in: *The Lesbian and Gay Studies Reader*, ed. Henry Abelove, Michele Barale, and David Halperin (New York: Routledge, 1993), 313ff.

cultural forms and everyday life are more connected than the fear of media influence communicates, it is also true that attachments to other kinds of narratives and characters matter.[14]

Yet media representations should not be interpreted as either constant throughout history, nor as all-encompassing truth. Instead, interventions on particular media, almost irrespective of their size, influence the dominant images that are communicated. Despite this caveat, cultural-historical residue from the past demonstrates a far-reaching degree of media consensus which, because of its dissemination, has developed a gravitas of significance that can only be overcome laboriously—and in this context, we need only think of the mass media depictions of queer communities during the last decades.[15]

Classic, queer economic well-being leans heavily on neoliberal, capitalist basic theses to provide orientation. Pursuing the goal of economic individualization—which stands for liberation in this case—several different feminist critiques of capitalism seem no longer to command majority appeal inside the postmodern and virtually interconnected queer community. The mechanisms of recognition, access to the "antechamber of power,"[16] and the possibility of participatory consumption have left deep marks behind them, which have been reaffirmed, and perhaps even reinforced, by the preponderant media image of recent decades.

Indeed, the present, queer pathos of emancipation seems to urgently require a move forward to a new stage, which is not only appropriate for the statistical, queer reality, and able to transfer this into self-confident political demands, but which can also direct itself towards those social movements in the twenty-first century that are socially critical. A

---

14   Linda Henderson, *Love and Money, Queer, Class, and Cultural Production*, (New York: 2013), 50ff.
15   See: "Larry Gross, What Is Wrong with This Picture? Lesbian Women and Gay Men on Television," in: *QueerWords, Queer Images, Communication and the Construction of Homosexuality*, ed. R. Jeffrey Ringer (New York: NYU Press, 1994), 143ff.
16   Martin J. Gössl, *Schöne, queere Zeiten? Eine praxisbezogene Perspektive auf die Gender und Queer Studies* (Bielefeld: transcript, 2014), 22.

comprehensive solidarity with queer communities from the most varied cultures, combined with a solidarity with other groups suffering under stigmatization and external labels would be just as essential and fruitful in this change of direction as integrating more strongly key global themes of societal politics: resource distribution and sustainability. The queer community has never been an island of interests unto itself, irrespective of where actors encounter the community, and in which cultural manifestation. It can ill afford to ignore the tumultuous seas engulfing it.

Queer prosperity is grounded in a community-based idea of prosperity, which must especially consider individual challenges and impasses, but also global ones. In facing up to this, the argument cannot be allowed to lead into an either-or situation, but must rather be understood as an intersectional moment. Sexual orientations and gender identities will continue to exert a strong influence on an individual biography, because even in the near future persecution, punishment, sentencing, and discrimination against queer people will continue to happen. And these threats are components of systems running through the whole of society, which is why a perspective is required that is both specific and holistic. From this perspective, it must matter how people consume or participate—exploitative labor conditions for a free, urban life, young people dropping out of school because of turbulent developments among children and teenagers, or an old age in poverty and isolation after years of political dislocations—all issues that acquire a different weight, when perceived from a queer perspective. This is why, as both microcosm and macrocosm, queer posterity must be thought about globally, comprehensively, and with solidarity. Such deliberations are prerequisites for leading queer successes on from the post-Stonewall, late twentieth century era, into the next stage. Just as vitally, this rethinking is needed to fuel innovation and developments in the twenty-first century.

4. Queer Success

He explains: "I started lifting weights when I was nine years old, for the diving. And that early impact ... It's like with gymnasts, it keeps everyone quite small." Daley shrugs, an Olympian whatevs. This is just one of those weird compromises – inexplicable and unacceptable to the rest of us – that Olympic athletes tend to make. ... Daley admits he has been criticised by some campaigners for continuing to enter competitions in countries where there is state-encouraged homophobia. "I go to Russia to compete quite often. I've competed in the Middle East. Lots of people would say, 'Boycott. Don't go.' But, do you know what? I think that going there, in a married relationship, and being able to compete, and climb on to a podium as a gay man – I think that speaks louder than boycotting. I think it shows we're real. Visible. I think it's powerful." ... So he steps to the edge of the concrete. "This is Tokyo. I will stand at the end of the board and be present. I'll breathe. I'll see my son and my husband in the audience. And that'll be enough."[1]

There are many kinds of success, and a greatly larger number of narratives of derailed biographies and initiatives. Areas in which we can be successful and receive recognition to match that success are manifold. Some of these areas correlate wonderfully to understandings of success shared by majorities in specific societies, while others necessitate a specific form of recognition. Not every successful human inevitably

---

[1] Tom Lamot and Tom Daley, "I'm only recognised when strangers think of me in my pants," in: *Guardian (US Edition)*, February 22, 2020, https://www.theguardian.com/sport/2020/feb/22/tom-daley-only-recognised-strangers-think-of-me-in-my-pants.

becomes a global household name. The parameters of success for those who do are definitely not automatically explicable.

Our opening quote is taken from an interview with Tom Daley, a British Olympian, who came out to a global public via a video platform in 2013.[2] This step gave the young athlete new renown beyond the borders of the diving community. It also made him known particularly, although not exclusively, in queer subculture. His achievements suddenly fell under an especially bright media spotlight, a development that inevitably prompted speculative comments on connections between his sexual orientation, his good looks, and his sporting success.

It is particularly sport, perhaps more than any other societal arena of achievement-based contention, which makes such honors special: distances, times, points, or specific strings of coordinated moves can be measured and compared easily. Sporting contests are played out under the watchful eyes of referees, and are accompanied by a media-based euphoria. Gradually, those who are successful continue to inch up the career ladder, in order to hopefully triumph by winning gold, that loveliest of all colors, at World Championships and Olympic Games.

The podium, the medal hung round ones neck, and the title and descriptive accolade to match, document these often-fleeting moments of being at the top. Which makes it even more important to conserve this fleeting fame in personal terms, to weld it to differing presentations of one's own personality. It's not only in sport that success can slip through one's fingers, whether through comparisons, a lack of respect being shown for success, or in the fickle transience of what media and public regard as sufficient achievement.

On several levels, Tom Daley can claim that he's experienced substantial success and specifically queer success. He's reached the very peak as a global sportsman, ensuring far-reaching recognition for his achievements from that section of the public informed about sport. Moreover, through coming out he appears to have widened further the circle of people who recognize his achievements, to include members of the public

---

2   Tom Daley, "Something I want to say ... ." Accessed November 1, 2023. https://www.youtube.com/watch?v=OJwJnoB9EKw.

who generally pay little regard to sporting events. Whether intentionally or unconsciously, he's managed to make his achievement visible: he has publicly connected his success with his own person.

One predicate for the recognition of that which is being exhibited is a counterpart or counterparts, who will register and value what is on show. However, a particular significance also must be accorded to that which is being presented and comprehended in any given societal space. In this fashion, queer success in the twenty-first century can justify itself through several of its facets. While doing so, it locates itself shockingly near—nearer than ever before—to ill-considered representational ideals of post-modernity: *achievement, love, and desire*.

The Merriam-Webster Dictionary defines "achievement" as "a result gained by effort: accomplishment."[3] Put more specifically, this definition links achievement with labor spent, experiencing strain, and a relatable result. Those results that correspond to heteronomous aims play a decisive role in what follows—regarding the recognition of success. The same applies to rewarding and acknowledging what has been achieved because of the result, i.e. a collective clarity in the context of exceptional goals. It rapidly becomes transparent that this form of determining achievement, which can be accessed through measurability, enjoys wide acceptance. This is how success in sport finds expression in units of time, or points, financial success through bank balances or employee numbers, and academic brilliance through titles and institutional affiliations. Yet we still must differentiate as to what motivates a particular achievement in the first place, whether a person is moved to act by "genuine fun in meeting a particular challenge, or because they want to reassure themselves regarding their own abilities, or because they want to avoid a specific failure that's looming."[4]

---

3   Entry for "achievement" in: *Merriam-Webster's Collegiate Dictionary* (Springfield, MA: Merriam-Webster, 2023). Retrieved November 1, 2023, fromhttps://www.merriam-webster.com/dictionary/achievement.

4   Thomas A. Langens, "Leistung," in: *Handbuch der Allgemeinen Psychologie – Motivation und Emotion*, ed. Veronika Brandstätter, Jürgen H. Otto (Göttingen: Hogrefe, 2009), 217n.

In 2009, shortly after the worldwide financial crisis, a female politician, little known until then, led by example during turmoil. Her successful interventions, a combination of achievement in the challenge of demonstrating one's own abilities, and the avoidance of a communal calamity, have gone down in history:

> Iceland's spectacular meltdown was caused by a banking and business culture that was buccaneering, reckless – and overwhelmingly male. ... . The crisis led to the downfall of the government and the prime minister's residence–which resembles a slightly over-sized white dormer bungalow–is now occupied by Jóhanna Sigurdardóttir, an elegant 66-year-old lesbian who is the world's first openly gay premier. When she lost a bid to lead her party in the 1990s, she lifted her fist and declared: "My time will come." Her hour has now arrived – and the same is true for a cadre of highly accomplished businesswomen.[5]

The media reception was unable to stave off the queer success shining through this story: Sigurdardóttir's biography touched people with its highs and lows, bound together with a mellow far-sightedness. The moment of political return was molded out of particular economic and apocalyptic circumstances, making it possible for her personal openness regarding her sexual orientation could seep through authentically, on the media plane and in societal politics. Jóhanna Sigurdardóttir was able to clock up this kind of success, and sudden recognition from wide swathes of the public, before her first activities in office—through years of steady achievement and through taking a chance to become prime minister of a nation-state rocked by crisis. From this point on, her actions would now not only be evaluated and relativized according to a general scheme, but also connected to her being a lesbian woman. Her success became a queer success, which the politician was also able to use

---

5   Ruth Sutherland, "After the crash, Iceland's women lead the rescue" in: *Guardian (US Edition)*, March 21, 2009. Accessed November 1, 2023. https://www.theguardian.com/world/2009/feb/22/iceland-women.

4. Queer Success   41

as such, when she married her long-term partner under the new law on same-gender marriage.⁶

After interest had been aroused in her person, the Icelandic politician's achievements were noticed and remarked on in much wider circles than before. Whether this was due to the economic crisis, her sexual orientation, or simply coincidence, Jóhanna Sigurdardóttir was discovered as a successful human by the public, even though the actual essence of what she had achieved remained unchanged. Interested observers bestowed the allure of queer success upon her as a politician and as a lesbian woman. The pathos of a queer pioneer was also pinned to her, a maneuver that provided the stage on which what she had achieved could be cherished. What she has accomplished is unquestionably impressive. There remains just as little doubt that she's been able to gain attention far beyond the borders of the northern island through details about her own individuality.

The second challenge to a generalizing way of perceiving success comes in the form of *Love*, which is substantial, eternal, or true by turns. The question posed thereby is no less complex than the question of how achievement is recognized:

> The Walt Disney complex, i.e. the search for the glimmering princess or prince, is exemplary, and deserves to be commented on. Despite critical scrutiny, the myth of "true" love remains, in utter accordance with cinematic models, and functions as an elementary matrix governing the enduring search for this heteronomous singularity. This can turn the search for a partner into a dream one has grown to love, and make search functions deteriorate into a product of one's own idealized notions, to a perfect fit, which must fulfill not only one's own interests and potentialities, but also that which an individual isn't able or willing to fulfill themselves.⁷

---

6   Reuters Staff, "Iceland's gay PM marries partner under new law," in: *Reuters*, June 28, 2010, https://www.reuters.com/article/idINIndia-49721320100628.
7   Martin J. Gössl, *Schöne, queere Zeiten?*, 114.

The forms that love and its heteronomous reception appears in are subject to diverse modalities of integration, in which media images, experiences, and role models influence how an individual shapes and values how they love. In this process, true love rapidly subjugates itself to a specific understanding of success, to the belief that the emotional connection between people can be classified as either successful or a failure. For many people in a virtually interconnected society, the fulfillment that stems from true love and the experience of a successful relationship has remained important, or has become even more important.[8]

Recent decades particularly have seen a shift in the queer perspective on success regarding love and relationships, a transformation that can be linked to changes in societal politics in the same period. The increasing legal equality of opportunity for same-gender partnerships is celebrated by many active representatives of queer communities—but as both boon and bane for these communities simultaneously. There's no place where this cognitive opposition has been expressed more publicly and clearly than in the UK in the third millennium:

> In Britain, legalizing gay marriage would be partly symbolic. Civil partnerships—passed under Prime Minister Tony Blair's Labor government—gave same-sex couples equal access to national pensions, inheritances, tax breaks and other rights enjoyed by married heterosexual couples. But Cameron, a Christian and married father of three whose position on same-sex marriage gradually evolved since winning the party's leadership in 2005, is calling gay marriage a matter of basic human rights. He is also making a pitch to uneasy religious conservatives, suggesting that the institution of marriage will reinforce traditional values of commitment and monogamy within the gay community.[9]

---

[8] See, for example, Silvia Fauck, *Mid Love Crisis, Beziehungstipps für Fortgeschrittene*, (Munich: Piper, 2020).

[9] Anthony Faiola, "British Conservatives lead charge for gay marriage (29.03.2012)," in: *Washington Post*, March 29, 2012, https://www.washingtonpost.com/world/british-conservatives-lead-charge-for-gay-marriage/2012/03/29/gIQAzatzjS_story.html.

The recognition of queer love is steered, via a road signposted as "equality of opportunity," toward a majoritarian ideal of society, which forces (queer) perspectives about success in love and relationships to change. Whether matching with a conservative understanding of the same or not, the centuries old concept of marriage—and the values that accrue to that—became part of the colonial norms of societal majorities, from which there is no escape. Films, books, poems, social media performances, and family traditions are all packed to the brim with omnipresent expectations concerning marriage, to which people can now subordinate queer permutations for relationships. It's on this stage that the new millennium individual moves, between societal recognition and social disorder. Furthermore, this third millennium human oscillates between success and neediness, and between idealized emotional success and the represented insufficiency of solitude:

> It is ironic that both sides acknowledge the limiting of bodies and relationships produced through Lawrence and same-sex marriage,[10] yet neither examines the debate from a standpoint of raced and classed queer liminality. The modernist time claims of queer theorists are not useful because, given the current progression of the political landscape, it is not possible to reclaim that kind of activism without accounting for the mainstreaming of gay and lesbian culture. Further, the mainstream can no longer ignore queer critiques of governmental regulation and the interrogation of bodies and relations. Because both sides point to the production of bodies that exist outside of the either/or framing of the debates, should we not start our examination of the issue from these bodies/relations that toe the line between queer and mainstream? Liminal bodies are those bodies that slip in and out of spaces, but are not fully acknowledged in either space. Further, because liminal bodies actualize slippage between categories, they highlight the ability to get beyond the either/or framing of the debate, while showing cracks in institutional frameworks-cracks that are potential sites of resistance. Examining bodies that occupy the

---

10   See: Dale Carpenter, "The Unknown Past of Lawrence v. Texas," *Michigan Law Review* 102, no. 7 (2004), https://doi.org/10.2307/4141912.

> raced and class liminal space between the queer and the mainstream will further open up the debate, allowing scholars and activists to account for those who are forced to the margins by both sides in the dichotomous debate.[11]

Indeed, the heteronormative structure at question here really is the true point of contention in understanding new queer articulations and the assumption of legal equality of opportunity. And these structures are proving themselves more obdurate than previously thought, especially in relation to their idealized consequences. Through these, queer love, the recognized and visible form of love, can now also be subdued by the imposition of a heteronormative grid. Thus, if further details come into play, queer love can be understood as classically "successful." Key details like monogamy, or eternal constancy if you prefer, can be quickly communicated, even if they can only be checked with difficulty, and much later in the day. So that suddenly, even if animated movies on the subject are a long time in coming, notions of a future like in a Walt Disney fairy tale become the dream of successful love, even for some in the queer community. In any case, this normative force runs rampant, strongly influencing those who allow themselves to be satisfied by applying traditional forms of relationships. These groups seem to spare hardly a thought for the curtailments that go hand in hand with such choices, or exclusions resulting from them.

The process of giving oneself up to *Desire*, the experience of a bodily and sensual connection with one or more others, often happens in the twenty-first century in ways never previously enacted in the history of humanity. Online platforms, established meeting points, urban diversity, and the Sexual Revolution taking place from 1968 have transformed sexual desire into something that's experienced in several dimensions:

---

11   Andrew Clark, "Falling through the Cracks: Queer Theory, Same-Sex Marriage, Lawrence v Texas, and Liminal Bodies," *disClosure: A Journal of Social Theory* 20, (2011), 40, https://doi.org/10.13023/disclosure.20.04.

> [These] changes are not about sex per se, but they all touch on key themes about the personal life. They suggest how the formality of sexual emotions, manners, language, groups and hierarchies of the past have become increasingly supplanted by more informal relations, so sexual patterns have been "deregulated." We now live in a world of sexual choices … , pure relationships … , cold intimacies … and disclosing intimacies … Tight codes and formal rules have given way to more fluid rules and a highly questionable set of choices about the personal life. A seeming "endless hunger for instant change," "self reinvention" and "short term living" have become themes which characterize the new personal—read also sexual—life.[12]

The actual possibilities for being able to perceive and experience one's own desire, also produce—far-removed from conventional structures—evaluation formats for successful or abortive transformation of desire. Both a desirous way of playing with oneself and the voluptuous connection with other people are under pressure from increasing idealizations:

> Popular media coverage may be sensationalistic, and undoubtedly influences attitudes and sexual behavior in adolescents and young adults. However, the hook-up phenomenon is not merely a creation of the media; rather, the media seems to be reflecting an actual shift in behavior. Such casual sexual experiences among college students are by no means a product of the 21st century; "one-night stands" and "casual sex" have been studied without the current "hook-up" context … . However, the high prevalence of these behaviors, coupled with an openness to display and discuss them, appears to be recent, particularly with respect to women … .[13]

---

12   Ken Plummer, "Critical Sexualities Studies," in: *The Wiley-Blackwell Companion to Sociology*, ed. G. Ritzer, (Hoboken: Wiley-Blackwell, 2011), https://doi.org/10.1002/9781444347388.ch14.

13   Chris Reiber and Justin R. Garcia, "Hooking up: Gender differences, evolution, and pluralistic ignorance," *Evolutionary Psychology* 8, no. 3, (2010): 391.

Sexual desire becomes one lively facet of an individual's life-performance, enabling that individual to put things into practice, visibly and resourcefully. Although many forms of desirous encounter are still encircled by taboo or weighed down by shame, the menacing fog emanating from a dirty cloud of attributions is starting to lift. Queer forms of desire, some of which have been cloaked in shame for smaller groups, others for many, are now split down the middle. This means that some experiences of queer desire are at least visible now, while other needs are still tabooed and thus in practice somewhat repressed. This sense of shame when faced with unbridled lust has not been, and cannot be—especially in the twenty-first century—reigned in, to remain exclusively within the bounds of same-genderness. As queer theoretician Michael Warner explains:

> Normalization and deviant shame. In modern culture the statistical and demographic imagination has created a new variety of shame. Norm of health and physicality are no longer understood to stem from divine plan ... . So I experience shame in the degree of my deviance from this imagined but essentially distributional norm. Queerness can be understood as the constitutive antithesis of modern demographic imaginary, and therefore in a sense as its unanticipated by-product.[14]

> Queer culture has practiced in countless ways the complexities not just of shame but of performances of shame, of formally mediated imitations of shah that objectify counternormative experience, of squirm-making disturbances in social field that bring counterpublics into a kind of public co-presence while also deploying shame to make a difference from the public. ... Staging shame as disruptions of relationality, we paradoxically create new relationships insofar as we can school ourselves not to be ashamed of our shame–a project that of

---

14 Michael Warner, "Pleasures and Dangers of Shame," in: *Gay Shame*, ed. David M. Halperin and Valerie Traub, (Chicago: University of Chicago Press, 2009), 291.

course disappears the second we persuade ourselves that not being ashamed of our shame requires us to be proud.[15]

Shame grounded in a societal perception of a queer otherness could transform itself, principally in the wake of the Stonewall Revolution, into a feeling of pride, whereby not only the personal but also desire was understood as a political and public substance. In the shadow of a series of conflicts in societal politics the idealization of successful desire—a sexuality of accomplishment—gained traction. This means that it's now no longer only people in queer communities who feel impacted by questions as to how their sex-life is doing, and through which means, or with whom, it can be enacted. The experience of desire has dared to make its way out of bedrooms and back rooms. To a point, it's left the admonitory conventions of previous ages behind it. Discovering one's own body and satisfying sexual appetites allows people to appear whole at least—or such, at least, is the perception of a modern form of faith. Sexual desire as *terra incognita* calls us to embark on journeys of discovery, challenges us to experiment, and wants intensive experiences in our one-off existences. Whoever abstains from vivacious desire seems to choose to go without fulfillment, consciously eschewing a successful saunter in the garden of sexual liberties.

Queer successes being oriented toward *achievement, love,* and *desire* reflects both a subcultural history and a normative standard. The capitalist understanding of achievement is continually offering the individual opportunities to clock up successes through their own hard-charging creative force. Or at least, this is the big capitalist story, and one which is still valid for many today:

> Economic inequalities have increased significantly in Germany. However, they are now accompanied by not more but less economic mobility. While, on the upper financial levels, a concentration of high incomes and wealth is taking place, supported by fiscal and tax politics to match, poverty is cementing itself dramatically at the lowest level.

---

15 Michael Warner, "Pleasures," 295n.

These polarizations in society's structure are embedded in an enduringly high inequality of opportunity in the German educational and vocational system. If recent tendencies of decreasing inequality of opportunity have been recorded recently, then these will have been conditioned by, if nothing else, a trend that has received little attention to date: the tendency of decreasing, or at least stagnating intergenerational aspirational mobility—which has happened concurrent to increasing downward social movements, particularly among the middle-classes.[16]

Even if successful achievements, viewed economically, are shaped by many factors—just like any other area of life—the fantasy of climbing socially as the result of one's own will power still seems catchy. All the more problematic seems the recognition that is extrapolated from that or, conversely, the allocation of guilt when success remains elusive.

It's precisely these factors that influence success that are such a challenge from a queer understanding of the subject, because an adolescence that "works," in psycho-social terms, an empowering education system, or one's authentic agency as a human can be impacted negatively by heteronormative parameters. Irrespective of whether it's an exhausting experience of coming-out at school, or parents with zero understanding for who one is, or the pressure to conform in a work-place setting: all these can function as individual, influencing factors, with consequences to match for an individual's everyday life. Perhaps it's precisely because of such biographical travails that queer success seems so illustrious, and maybe societal circumstances in recent decades have made it more illustrious still: imagine an individual actually mastering something, despite everything. Nonetheless, isolated examples of success should not delude neither a general nor a queer subculture regarding the extent and profundity of still existing queer challenges, however important the statues provided by such cases are. On both macro and micro levels, it's not at all easy to be forced into diagnosing a difference between oneself and the

---

16 Olaf Groh-Samberg and Florian R. Hertel, "Ende der Aufstiegsgesellschaft?" *APuZ aktuell, Aus Politik und Zeitgeschichte* 65, (October 2015), 31.

majority. Yet for so many individuals, such differences are relevant, as they precipitate radical, biographical ruptures.

> Most homeless youth have histories of family disruption, abuse, and family substance use … . LGBT status, although not necessarily the proximal cause of homelessness, is correlated with higher risk of many factors associated with homelessness, such as victimization at home and at school … Some homeless youth were "kicked out" and others actually chose to leave because of conditions they could no longer tolerate …[17]

Achievement, love, and desire as one form in which queer success manifests may sound like a rather slick major chord, but the success in question is partly autonomous, partly heteronomous. A lack of self-determination particularly can precipitate precarious personal circumstances—potentially becoming homeless, or dropping out of school, are stark illustrations of this phenomenon. The same absence of autonomy also encourages some individuals to retreat into a heteronormative farce. Both moments, precarization and retreat, deflate the egalitarian nature of queer success as a catchall concept. Mindful of this, the open question of what queer success should actually be about must be answered elsewhere.

Queer success necessitates both individual and collective perspectives, capable of giving an account of the aforementioned circumstances surrounding the multiple factors that influence queer life. Normative value systems are permanently in flux, but are nonetheless applied in a variety of ways. From these emerge multidimensional biographies of queer individuals, of whom some, despite all obstacles, build accomplished lives, or even existences that societal majorities interpret as successful. Other individuals, who have undergone the same pressures from normative values, have no choice but to endure existential crises.

---

17 Geoffrey L. Ream and Nicholas Forge, "Homeless lesbian, gay, bisexual and transgender (LGBT) youth in New York City: Insights from the field," *Child Welfare* 93, no. 2 (2014): 10.

Such impasses, which appear to be written into the cultural code of queer communities, call out for social responsibility to be taken for fair development opportunities, and grounded social care. Moreover, what's needed is a lived openness for many varieties of love in all their consensually celebrated forms, but without imposing historical, or majority-backed idealizations onto queer people. True success is to be found here in the self-determination of an individual person, in the creation of a shared basis of two or more people, and in the authentic experience of one's own desirous imaginations. People are all too quick to judge—a daily danger in queer communities, as in non-queer ones—anything seen as either too far-out, or too conventional. The allure of beautiful success stretches itself out sinuously over many areas of life, and often reproduces itself abundantly. Idealizations articulated by third persons can be the consequences of such reproduction, which can lead to a further exaltation of achievement, love, and desire. All too eagerly, a common next step involves drawing comparisons and analyzing apparent deficits: less success, no relationship, or an unconventional form of sexual longing, and the grand facade of recognition already begins to crumble. But it's precisely in the multifariousness of the facades that the fruitful difference between success and queer success lies. This is a nexus where, in consequence, unconventional forms of showing esteem are celebrated. Whether polyamory, leather fetishism, or simply jobs that earn people a living—none of these should be viewed as a label for exterior perceptions of queer success: and all the less so, when the task in hand is actually considering a holistic picture of a queer biography. As long as heteronormative processes of socialization impact negatively on queer individuals, majority-based grids for evaluating success will have a substantially distorting effect on queer biographies—even leaving aside the overall fact that the patterns through which we judge the success of others are far from being fair. That's why it matters for a queer subculture to respond critically when required—even if it might prefer to bask in the recognition that majorities are finally granting it. And this is required on all occasions when individuals are turned into laughing stocks, or pressurized into socially invisible realms. Both these forms are all too familiar mechanisms for maintaining systems of labeling and stigmatization, which should leave nobody in the queer community cold.

Queer success is about mastering the challenge of developing an emphatic life in a community that openly shows esteem for an individual's closest companions and other acquaintances—and for all the potentialities these people have.

5. Queer Diversions

A subcultural community's artistic express can constantly draw on its own forms and standards, in order to create specific narratives. In so doing, the conversation can be conducted either with a heteronormative society, or about the same, and be authored by queer and non-queer people alike. Even *the* location of gay liberation, the Stonewall Inn, which symbolized queer recreation in that period, was planned, built and run by the local mafia—i.e. by non-queer people.[1]

Queer entertainment encompasses silent pleasures like books and paintings alongside more visible expressions, including music, bars, clubs, and perform. It reflects itself at the level of the personal, in jokes, how people are addressed, innocuous-seeming conversational topics, and much more. Queer diversion functions as a meeting point, as an experience of what one has in common. Understood in this way, it's no twentieth century invention, but rather one with deeper historical roots. It should be added that queer entertainment is only formalized, or a component of productions, in some of its means of expression. It's much more common for queer interactions to be expressed in everyday situations, which follow a looser, less formal script. This cultural template can be broken down, within a queer culture, into subcultural narratives, can intermittently draw on international codes—through, for example, popular cult figures in public life—but can also demonstrate regional specifics. Queer diversions turn up to an equal extent in both public and

---

1   David Carter, *Stonewall, The Riots that sparked the Gay Revolution* (New York: Macmillan 2004), 79ff.

private spaces, and can be continually produced and reproduced—if this is what the participants present want and are able to set in motion:

> Gay culture can refer to new works of literature, film, music, art, drama, dance, and performance that are produced by queer people and that reflect on queer experience. Gay culture can also refer to mainstream works created mostly by heterosexual artists, plus some (closeted) queer ones, that queer people have selectively appropriated and reused for anti-heteronormative purposes.[2]

At the end of his pioneering work on the reality of *How to be Gay*,[3] the American queer theoretician David Halperin attempts to define gay culture. But his attempt to do so without an overarching queer principle is somewhat off target. His bid references a broad understanding of the persons involved, by finding articulations for queer people and their reflections of queer experiences, although his investigative methods have also enabled contributions from non-queer persons: in history, as today. Moreover, Halperin concludes that this form of culture, or sub-culture, is an essential factor in the queer community both before and since Stonewall:

> It is clear that traditional gay male culture—that is, subculture—continues to provide queers of all sorts with emotional, aesthetic, even political resources that turn out to be potent, necessary, and irreplaceable. The open and explicit gay male culture produced by gay liberation has not been able to supplant a gay male subculture, grounded in gay identification with non-gay forms, or to substitute for it an original gay male culture grounded in the vicissitudes of gay identity. The impetus driving much gay cultural production still springs less from gay existence than from gay desire.[4]

---

2 David M. Halperin, *How to be Gay* (Cambridge, Massachusetts: Belknap Press, 2012), 421.
3 Halperin, *How to be Gay*.
4 Halperin, *How to be Gay*, 427.

The culture in question here is not merely a part of queer diversion, but also a logical form of expression. It's queer forms of interaction that create a cultural feeling of belonging to a group in the first place, and thus express belonging. Many of these forms have remained unpopular codes, provoking little interest among societal majorities. But this seems to have changed, at least partly, with the end of the twentieth century and the coming of the twenty-first. Not only are series, films, books, and theater plays one part of a greater reception of (queer) entertainment: increasingly, they can now be experienced in the very essence of this subculture:

> When it debuted on TV, *Will & Grace*[5] was revolutionary. Not only was it the first mainstream LGBTQ sitcom on TV, but it was one in which gay life was portrayed in a naturalistic way; ... Television–particularly on cable and streaming sites–has changed exponentially in the 20 years since the show began, with a myriad of diverse representations of the LGBTQ community ...[6]

These subcultural insights, contextualized within the framework of a broad public, evidently affect queer labeling and stigmatization. Beyond that, amusing cultural forms such as these have the capacity to change the norms and ideals held by majorities. It's particularly television and internet images that extend, repress, form, and abbreviate queer perception patterns and their respective expectations. In so doing, normative parameters of the societal majority continue to be formative, for example in questions of how much intimacy and skin is allowed to be shown, or how explicit dialogues are allowed to become, but no one's claiming that the walls of the permissible cannot be shifted. Rather, these boundaries are mostly left unarticulated in the negotiation process—apart, that is, from clear legal stipulations—because media

---

5   *Will & Grace* was an American TV series that ran from 1998–2020. "Will & Grace," IMDB, accessed November 8, 2023, https://www.imdb.com/title/tt0157246/.
6   Jane Mulkerrins, "'We had death threats': the defiant return of Will & Grace," in: *Guardian (US Edition)*, January 20, 2018, https://www.theguardian.com/culture/2018/jan/20/we-had-death-threats-the-defiant-return-of-will-grace.

formats count on generating interest and not disapproval amongst the target audience: this can, in the case of early evening programming, be the general mass of viewers. Programmers aim for precisely this fine line between social disgust and witty surprises. Despite this is tightrope act, the whole premise that the format aims at is a comprehensive success. The thinness of this line also encompasses the boundary, vital in subcultural terms, of whether audiences laugh with a TV character, or about him.

Since the start of the millennium, further queer formats have been able to establish themselves in a generally perceptible context. In so doing, these formats have placed specific facets of a queer subculture in the public spotlight. Media-based processes during recent decades also clearly exemplify how rapidly notions of adequate entertainment have changed in postmodern, virtually interconnected societies. Or, as an alternative summary: how strongly the virtualization of media formats was able to conquer global markets, and subcultural target groups—and how this virtualization influences, in turn, societal imaginations:

> Through Drag Race, the language of drag is not just gaining recognition by a wider public–it is being turned into a new art form through memes, GIFs, and content that floods millions of people's social media feeds. ... On Drag Race, language stops being just subcultural "lingo" and is a vehicle for spreading and popularizing drag slang, which is heavily used, explained, and commented on during the show and subsequently adopted by pop culture.[7]

Drawing from a particular kind of New York ballroom dancing scene,[8] the artist and performer RuPaul created a series format, which had what it takes to blow queer boundaries and heteronormative ideas to the wind.

---

7   Carolina Are, "How 'RuPaul's Drag Race' changed the way we speak" (02.10.2019), in: *Quartz*, October 2, 2019, https://qz.com/quartzy/1715788/how-rupau ls-drag-race-made-lgbtq-culture-mainstream/.

8   Presented, for example, in: Jennie Livingston, *Paris is Burning* (Documentary film, 1990), available on IMDB, https://www.imdb.com/title/tt0100332/.

5. Queer Diversions   57

His *Drag Race* pulled drag performance, one segment of queer performance culture, onto center stage, a position from which it has enjoyed uncanny levels of media popularity ever since. Drag performance, which has not always been appreciated lovingly within queer subculture, has gone on from here to achieve cult status. This status is expressed in the most various ways, by a spectrum of artists of all genders—and amusement always remains at the heart of this entertainment format:

> Much of the openly gay-themed culture that has emerged since Stonewall continues to share the revolutionary goals of gay liberation. Its originality, artistic experimentation, and sheer brilliance are very far removed from the standard gay identity politics of the mainstream gay movement. But that genuinely inventive gay culture has suffered the same fate as the identity-based culture that emerged in the same period, insofar as both seem to arouse in gay audiences a similar sense of tedium. It is as if contemporary gay people have a hard time distinguishing truly original, innovative queer work from the comparatively trite, politically earnest, in-group cultural productions that you find on the Logo[9] Channel.[10]

Indeed David Halperin, who I've already cited in previous chapters, thinks that media representations of queer contents in today's world threaten to make queer, creative inventive richness banal. It's an open question whether Halperin is right in this assertion. But it's indisputable that RuPaul's show format, and the queer contents which this stages, certainly exert a profound influence on postmodern queer communities, and on society in general.[11]

---

9   "Logo is a television and digital entertainment brand inspired by and for the LGBTQ+ community. From entertainment to activism, Logo features one-of-a-kind personalities, shows, specials, and stories with a distinctly queer lens." Logo's description of itself, on: *YouTube*, last accessed X November, 2023, https://w ww.youtube.com/user/LogoTV/about.
10 David Halperin, *How to be Gay*, 428.
11 See: Cameron Crookston, ed., *The Cultural Impact of RuPaul's Drag Race* (Chicago: University of Chicago Press, 2021).

We can say, and therein lies the viable compromise implicit in David Halpern's appraisal, that queer amusement is subject to constant and permanent social influences, which can emanate from the queer community itself, but also, evidently, from far-reaching trends, or popular measures. Gay Liberation in Manhattan in 1969 had, for example, a genuinely fundamental influence on which forms and structures pertaining to a queer subculture were then relayed to a wider public. In his dissertation on the queer economy in New York City, historian Christopher Mitchell concludes:

> [Q]ueer people themselves—as the central entrepreneurs, displacing the older system of the closet economy in which straight outsiders, typically under the aegis of organized crime, dominated. As a movement that has occurred largely within markets, Gay Liberation and liberalization is a remarkable achievement for a social group whose very emergence was defined by and limited to stigmatized and criminalized markets. However, the history of the market also suggests some important limitations.[12]

Queer amusement of that period underwent a radical transformation, which must ultimately be traced back to changes in societal systems and politics. However, such transformations in queer life are a continuous development, which makes a moment or period of fixity seem impossible. Queer recognition of wanted and high-demand entertainment forms has altered constantly, and fitted into the givens of any particular period or place. It would be wrong to believe that queer illegality could completely prevent queer amusements happening, or that global interconnections could not also unleash their impacts in those regions of the world, in which queer life in everyday culture can be threatened with strong repressive measures.

---

12 Christopher A. Mitchell, "The Transformation of Gay Life from the Closet to Liberation, 1948–1980: New York City's Gay Markets as a Study in Late Capitalism," (PhD diss., Rutgers, State University of New Jersey, 2015), 408.

> [T]he creation of a public discourse of gay pride and the practice of "coming out" enervated the power of anti-gay stigma to constrain gay social, cultural, economic, and ultimately political activities. Rather than a successive chronology, my framework views this long period of liberalization as one in which the market-based aims of liberalization and the more politically intersectional and transformative aims of Gay Liberation overlapped and sometimes competed. ... If, as my introduction suggests, the more recent past has been characterized by the collapse of the local gay market, then it behooves activists and thinkers in the LGBTQ movement to look not only at the ways in which market strategies can help us to break down the barriers of racial, gender, and economic justice as well as the ways in which those strategies have been incommensurate to the task.[13]

And it would be truly pointless to deny this shift. There's been a substantial decrease in the number of establishments in New York's queer bar scene, which has been celebrated for decades far beyond the city boundaries:

> While all gay bar listings declined by 36.6 percent between 2007 and 2019, the number of listings for bars serving people of color declined by 59.3 percent, cruisy men's bar listings declined by 47.5 percent, and bars for women declined by 51.6 percent. Discussions of gay bar closures should pay attention to those LGBT communities at greatest risk of losing their places.[14]

This is a transition that runs through entire queer neighborhoods, which have crystallized in urban centers across most of the globe. But attempts to put the brakes on this trend have had little success to date:

> Some worry about cities losing prominent cultural identities as neighborhoods shrink, even to the point of suggesting municipal

---

13   Christopher Mitchell, *The Transformation*, 409.
14   Greggor Mattson, "Are Gay Bars Closing? Using Business Listings to Infer Rates of Gay Bar Closure in the United States, 1977–2019," *Socius: Sociological Research for a Dynamic World* 5, (2019): 2, https://doi.org/10.1177/2378023119 894832.

> interventions such as rent controls. But the shift appears to be happening organically as cities and societies undergo a variety of changes, and even the best-intentioned government interventions have the potential to backfire. Municipal leaders largely seem to be working with the changing neighborhoods and embracing the progress and innovation that comes with more integrated cities.[15]

Indeed, social change in a queer community cannot be artificially delayed and is, exemplified in the histories recounted in the above, a continuous process. Demand, in the early twenty-first century, for queer amusement as a core ingredient of recognizable neighborhoods, is lower than in preceding decades. The experiencing of omnifarious queer social needs, and concrete wishes and demands for queer and amusing ways to spend free time, has largely moved into the omnipresent virtual sphere: accessible any place, any time.

Virtual dating platforms make getting to know people via one's cellphone or computer easy, and ordering queer-specific products online is equally straightforward. Analogue dates arising from such digital encounters take place in liberal—although not specifically queer—settings, or relocate to the private sphere.

This queer-cultural transformation, which has barely been reflected on in some quarters, can unleash questionable ramifications, particularly when the marginalization of queer individuals in structuring any kind of entertainment and its reception—especially in the context of queer entertainment—fosters negative associations:

> But it's an unavoidable truth that the rise in cultural representation in the US and UK is also at odds with the lived experience of many LGBTQ+ people. The last 10 years might have brought with them new legislative freedoms–but these have been met with a backlash, including a shocking rise in hate crime on both sides of the Atlantic. ... As

---

15   Katie Pyzyk, "The disappearance of the modern-day 'gayborhood'," in: *Smart Cities Dive*, November 7, 2017, https://www.smartcitiesdive.com/news/the-disa ppearanc e-of-the-modern-day-gayborhood/510134/.

capitalism tightens its grip on queer stories, we should pay close attention to the type of LGBTQ+ stories that are becoming marketable—and also who is benefitting from the way that these stories are being told. While culture might appear to be embracing LGBTQ+ stories, if it fails to embrace LGBTQ+ creators too, then this decade's queer awakening might end up being "just a phase."[16]

Discrepancies certainly can result in the tension between the reproduction of reality, and real circumstances. When the queer ideal assumes entirely other forms in everyday life, so that images transmitted by the media have merely a partial effect—or none at all—then a danger arises: a deceptive illusion of recognition can mislead people regarding the genuine depths of influential attributions. This can influence individuals that could and want to be part of any kind of entertainment, but don't match with the arbitrary ideals pertaining to these. Moreover, these deceptions can become a tough, quotidian experience for all those who cannot, or don't want to fulfill the clichés they're suddenly confronted with.

Spatial and emotional distances within a queer neighborhood may be to blame for this individualization process. Swaps are made, whereby community activities, and a collective sense of being together, are exchanged for opportunities to structure one's own life. Because it can be understood as a "law of nature," that individuals have only a limited time on earth to fulfil their needs, many forms of real entertainment remain unused and ignored in our modern era. The virtual collective appears to provide sufficient fulfillment, and what's on offer in the field of queer entertainment, and the welcome side effects accompanying such pursuits—fun, love, friendship, and sex—exist merely as phenomena for an occasional weekend. In so doing, the autonomously led organization of private relationships, as a part of free individualization, alters not only

---

16 Louis Staples, "Did culture really embrace queer people this decade?" on *BBC Culture*, December 26, 2019, https://www.bbc.com/culture/article/20191218-th e-de cade-that-saw-queerness-go-mainstream.

the collectivity of real queer communities, but also the classic configurations of social constructs, including family and partnership:

> However, alongside this, there was also strong evidence amongst the people interviewed of a set of interrelated relationship practices that served reparatively to suture the selves undone by processes of individualization. These practices can be understood as counter-heteronormative, in that they challenged the dominant heterosexual model of personal relationships that values and privileges the co-residential conjugal couple relationship above all others. These practices were: the prioritizing of friendship, the de-centring of sexual/love relationships, and the forming of non-conventional partnerships. ... This meant that very few people constructed the sexual/love relationship as the exclusive space of intimacy in their lives, and indeed for many it was not even the primary space of intimacy. This de-centring of the sexual/love relationship was understood self-reflexively by many interviewees as consequent on the experience of divorce or the ending of a long-term cohabiting relationship; the pain and disruption this caused was seen as giving rise to a new orientation to relationships—the linked downplaying of sexual/love relationships and the increased valuing of friendships.[17]

Based on this qualitative analysis, I can articulate a suspicion: communities of interest, centered on the agency of queer collectives, are not alone in experiencing a symbolic form of anti-solidarity. Beyond this, such communities now only play a partial role—if any role at all—in the perceptions of a queer individual.

The queer cultures that lie behind such communities—in a trend comparable to the cultures of relevant NGOs—are increasingly being lost, together with their regional, social, and societal politics components. When they are kept alive, this labor is carried out by just a few, an endeavor with more chance of success when grants and membership

---

17   Sasha Roseneil, "Queer Individualization: The Transformation of Personal Life in the Early 21st Century," *NORA—Nordic Journal of Women's Studies* 15, no. 2–3 (2007): 92n, https://doi.org/10.1080/08038740701482952.

fees ensure support their continued operations, and they don't rely solely on turnover.

Are we threatened with the end of a diverse queer entertainment scene? Or, and possibly worse, its exclusive reduction to experiences of sexuality?

> Of all the men going to sex venues, 75 % went to public cruising areas and 61 % to baths. We found that 39 % of men who went to sex venues went only to public cruising areas (cruisers), 25 % went only to baths (bathers), and 36 % went to both types of venues (multi-venue users). The demographic characteristics of the men were similar across the 3 possible patterns of venue use, although men younger than 26 years and men older than 55 were more likely to be cruisers (50 % and 57 %, respectively) than were men in their mid-20s to mid-50s (33 %–46 %).[18]

Despite the virtual options, physical and sexually entertaining locations are demonstrating an impressive tenacity. Several different arguments could provide explanations for this: earlier convictions, that an individual could operate anonymously online, have been taken down several pegs, by a growing and general awareness about data protection issues. On the other hand, nigh on unerring profiles of desire can be extracted from virtual behavior patterns, which can compromise and disadvantage precisely those individuals who want queer sex and sexuality, but don't want to join a queer community. Moreover, certain groups opting out of virtual sexuality realms means that those deciding to subject themselves to heteronomous or autonomous virtual representation accumulate a critical potential that's larger than other groups have, but also more vulnerable. There are also considerable numbers who regard such virtual abbreviations, the reduction of oneself to just a few labels, and the self-marketing that goes with it, as a mystery, or simply

---

18   Diane Binson, William J. Woods, Lance Pollack, Jay Paul, Ron Stall, and Joseph A. Catania, "Differential HIV Risk in Bathhouses and Public Cruising Areas," *American Journal of Public Health* 91, no. 9 (2001): 1484, https://ajph.aphapublications.org/doi/10.2105/AJPH.91.9.1482.

unsatisfying. In any case: while virtual forms of getting to know people do work for large numbers—user statistics speak for themselves—the physical consolidation of these encounters still requires real spaces to be put into practice: such spaces are usually shared, or only available within the framework of tight-knit social groupings. Beyond this, a virtual initiation into a new relationship can take much longer, because the personal situations of the interested parties can remain unknown to the other for long, or because mobility, under particular circumstances, hardly seems possible. And this without even providing an account of the power with which social media reduces individuals down to a couple of pictures, which, when swapped between persons, leads to decisions, taken within seconds, about whether a meeting is desired, even possible, or has already been ruled out. Users of queer, sexual amusement locations are spared some of this hassle, because the location, a shared time, and by and large a shared motivation—why one's come to the location in the first place—seem to be unequivocal. With this background, it won't surprise readers to hear that such locations that are happy to facilitate their users paying in cash, and know how to protect their customers' anonymity.

Yet doubts remain. Can and should the whole gamut of queer entertainment in postmodern and virtually interconnected societies really be reduced to sex alone? I presented an initial response to this question at a 2017 conference:

> Backrooms and darkrooms still exist, and are still being set up anew. First because there are still many men without options of intimate sexual contacts in their everyday heteronorm-designed life, and second, queer culture is inevitable pinned on sexual desire. Same-sex intimacy is, unnecessary what intensity, something "different." Every space where this intimacy can happen without disappointing social concepts of normality, are decent for all queer-defined people at many steps in their lives. Moreover observing the social interaction in back/darkrooms it becomes clear that such spaces are much about an egalitarian understanding on basic principles of sexual attraction, where – because of the non-conformity of this rooms – other social

and informal customs, bias or social rules are not that relevant in a Bourdieu'ish self-understanding and self-representation. Comparing to the all-embracing heteronormativity, back/darkrooms are perhaps spaces of impossibility of living queer companionship and intimacy.[19]

Spaces that have a primary connection to sexuality are genuinely more than merely locations of desire. Rather, these zones provide possibilities for queer-social interactions, which detach themselves, markedly, from a heteronormative understanding of space, and thus open up spaces for gender and sexual diversity. These geographical points have been, and remain, often places with traditions of consistently providing options for activities/modes of being that have been condemned socially in many locations. These niches of queer freedom have been and still are tightly defined bubbles, which must house an incredible amount, and endure, in the smallest physical spaces imaginable. That said, what is self-evident about them often shoves its way into the foreground of etic perceptions: sexuality.

But such exclusive forms of perceiving would do both queer locations and queer amusement an injustice—focusing too narrowly on the self-evident here covers up a wealth of significant facets. Of course, gender and sexuality build a strong connection between those present in a queer context, but this doesn't necessarily mean that one singular intention informs this attendance. Instead, a plurality of motivations join together, which make such spaces seem exclusive: verbal and cultural exchanges, being how one is, getting to know people, or the wish to spend a few minutes with kindred spirits, for whom what is usually one's own seems so utterly normal. The queer amusement happening at such locations is, in community terms, broader, and socially deeper, than people think, and is thus closer to the miscellany of variegated human needs than I suspected when I began these deliberations.

---

19 Martin J. Gössl, "Dark/Backrooms: The Meaning of Queer Spaces of Sex" (unpublished Conference Paper given on November 3, 2017). https://www.researchgate.net/publication/328686195.

In this light, it makes sense that certain forms of entertainment, image, and language are deeply anchored in almost any form of queer amusement. Whether we're talking about drag culture, displaying naked skin covered only by limited clothing (worn by both guests and staff), political discourse pertinent to the subjects at hand, the commonplace and visible screening of queer pornos, rapid wit and banter that hits its targets, the discarding of gender-based normativity in behavior, the omnipresence of HIV, and much, much more: queer amusement provides space for all these elements. In specifying certain elements, and in projects counter to heteronormativity, queer entertainment is a lived, performative activity—not at all times and everywhere, of course, but certainly interpreted in terms of superordinated significance—to quench not only sexual desire, but also individuals' needs to be in a collective, queer, cultural world. While this queer cultural normality may occasionally serve profane forms, these very same forms contribute to the construction of a different normality. This is what makes it inappropriate to judge the quality of such cultural offerings. Queer entertainment, and the locations at which this happens, are synonymous with political and historical spaces. This subculture has had no choice but to establish itself within the confines of the possible—and under the circumstances prevailing in any given era. Even when particular large media-based productions do get a positive, and queer-cultural reception in the perceptions of the general public—and this is unquestionably welcome—local structures remain essential, in terms of the specificity of their provision, and thereby subject to other rules. A general appreciation of queer intimacy, closeness, and distance is still subject to a heteronormative foundational structure in postmortem and virtually interconnected societies. In some locations, this structure can be left behind, at least for a while, so that these locations can provide real alternatives. A queer community cannot turn its back on queer-media formats, and queer-regional niches—even when the particulars of what's on offer aren't to everybody's taste.

6. Queer Sexuality

Shifts in scientific treatises about sexuality, and lived, expressed forms of sexuality themselves, have not simply been slow and continuous during the last two centuries, but are also impacted by radical transformations in society and its politics—the culture of sex, and its history, can't be understood as a continuum. Both first and second-wave feminism, same-gender desire becoming visible in the nineteenth century, the Social Revolution of 1968, and the Stonewall Revolution in 1969, are only the most vivid examples of this historical process. The human body, and the sexuality that resides therein, were gauged anew, and incorporated into a medical, legal, social, cultural, and political discourse, each time with the aim of adding more knowledge and clarity, about historical, spiritual, and moral interpretations, to the bodily, gender-based, and sexual ensemble. Now that many actors have arrived in the twenty-first century, many aims appear to have been achieved, and clarity to prevail, about what defines heteronormativity, and who, based on which genders and which sexualities, may be categorized as "queer." Yet this categorical definiteness is now increasingly dissolving again, as individuals flee regularly from the segments laid down in the past, or claim lifestyles for themselves that could be interpreted as both conservative *and* queer. The stage of queer sexuality is like a street party that grows ceaselessly, with countless new forms displaying new wares. This is a festival where new possibilities, forming at the margins and complementing each other, can always be discovered:

> "No matter what label you end up sticking with," Watson explains, "It's also important to know that your attractions and identities can be fluid and change." It's why Alfred Kinsey, a famous sexologist, invented the Kinsey scale – a numbered spectrum between completely homosexual and completely heterosexual – to help queer people express how they felt. Because even in 1948, people were realizing that no two bisexuals loved and desired people in the same exact way, and that sexuality evolves.[1]

Indeed, measuring queer sexuality as a defined territory is genuinely difficult, even when many seem to know what could be meant by it. The fluid and inconstant character trait of queer sexuality is what makes it impossible to fence it in—or to fence other people out. It's in debt to this reality that obligatory terms like LGBTI[*2] or specific descriptions like lesbian/gay do their work, in order to hit the spot for communication purposes. This makes sense because cultural and political discourses, but above all scholarly and scientific studies and knowledge production requires an unerring terminology, so conclusions can be reached, or value added in comparison to the starting points of such investigations. "Queer" functions as a catchall term, a theoretical model, which allows the theme as a whole to remain in view, but within which specifics are threatened with loss. Queer sexuality can be named as a holistic, social-cultural construct, and worked through in this way, but what is special about it is, unerringly, individual desire and personal expression:

> Americans are becoming more accepting in their views of LGBT people and homosexuality in general, and the number of people identifying as LGBT has grown in recent years. For example, 63 % of Americans said in 2016 that homosexuality should be accepted by society,

---

1   Caroline Colvin, "Am I Queer? Here's How To Tell, According To Sexuality Experts," in: *elite daily (Bustle Digital Group)*, August 19, 2019, https://www.elite daily.com/p/am-i-queer-heres-how-to-tell-according-to-sexuality-experts-18 649786. For more on Courtney Watson, the female psychotherapist in Oakland, USA, referred to by Colvin, see: http://www.doorwaytherapeutics.com/about/.
2   LGBTI* and LGBTI+: Lesbian, Gay, Bisexual, Trans, Inter and more.

compared with 51 % in 2006. LGBT adults recognize the change in attitudes: About nine-in-ten (92 %) said in a 2013 Pew Research Center survey of adults identifying as LGBT that society had become more accepting of them in the previous decade.[3]

A study conducted by the Pew Research Center, 2017, concluded that there had been an increase in persons identifying as LGBT, from 8.3 million adults in the USA in 2012, to 10.1 million in 2017.[4]

Such statistics make evident one of the many reasons why categorizations are a necessity: without descriptive definitions, transparent conclusions are difficult, become a matter of conjecture, or a simply impossible. If these clear links to the subcultures cannot be established, insightful images pertaining to a queer community, and norms of majority-based structures, would remain opaque. That's why queerness as a descriptor requires structures, which can make visible gender-based and sexual identity as a minority, as smaller groups within larger ones, as a cultural and social concept, as particular historical content, and much more. Parallel to this, queerness can also mirror the individual level—one's own queer desire and queer sexuality—especially when established self-descriptive terms seem to fit badly, or aren't even on offer in the first place.

Alongside the diversity of desire and expression of gender-based relations pertaining to it, queer sexuality is also the conceptual home for questions of putting into practice, or applying theories. Because this other form of sexuality and gender can indeed, parallel to a conventional norm, be lived out in practice through a spectrum of facets, and at equally diverse locations. That said, not all modes of experiencing are equally popular, or have the same amount of prestige accorded to them. The appraisal of queer sexuality from without—by a majority united through norms—and from within—by a queer, sub-community, the

---

3   Anna Brown, "5 key findings about LGBT Americans," *Pew Research Center*, June 13, 2017, https://www.pewresearch.org/fact-tank/2017/06/13/5-key-findingsabout-lgbt-americans/.
4   Brown, "5 key findings."

components of which are constantly differentiating themselves from each other—cause hierarchies of recognition. As early as 1993, the American cultural anthropologist Gayle Rubin labeled this phenomenon the "hierarchy of sex," in an anthology article.[5]

This hierarchization impacts on the perception and experience of sexuality in general, the representation of gender, the kind of desire, and the creativity with which the satisfaction of a particular desire is put into practice. Irrespective of whether the desire in question is queer or nonqueer, the pattern of traditions is extremely familiar, and has been abundantly interpreted. In media and in schools, in countless magazines, in public life, and in the community: all these communicate finely made excerpts of sexual acceptance, while never, or hardly ever, finding concrete words to name the sex itself:

> In this sense, taboos can be understood as a system of norms, as the morals and morality of a society, and thus as the expression of societal power that's joined to the same. This societal power is divine, or, we could say, taboo, so that it cannot, in itself, be called into question, or changed. As a sacred power for cultural concepts about the "rightness" of specific, societal notions, this power inscribes itself on and into the individual body, by means of societal notions about gender and sexuality, which can be rewritten as taboos. The individual body then internalizes these societal ideas in the form of its conscience. Thus, notions about taboos are culturally specific symbols of societal power, which cling to the bodily.[6]

This "bad" conscience induces a sense of shame, and the shame results in a taboo. This powerful form of self-control exerts strong pressure on sex-

---

5   Gayles S. Rubin, "Thinking Sex: Notes for a Radical Theory of the Politics of Sexuality," in *The Lesbian and Gay Studies Reader*, ed. Henry Abelove, Michele Aina Barale and David M. Halperin, (New York: Routledge, 1993), 3ff.

6   Lidia Guzy, "Tabu–Die kulturelle Grenze im Körper," in: *Geschlecht als Tabu: Orte, Dynamiken und Funktionen der De/Thematisierung von Geschlecht*, ed. Ute Frietsch, Konstanze Hanitzsch, Jennifer John, and Beatrice Michaelis (Bielefeld: transcript, 2008), 19n.

ual modes of behavior and gender-based identities to find forms of tolerance and acceptance that are worthy of being applied. With these givens, queer sexuality must routinely sit down at the societal negotiating table. By turn, it is defined by those who are currently doing the negotiating, and by the details of how desires should and could be satisfied. One can't help but think of a certain social and dynamic capriciousness, which cannot simply be denied. In practice, general societal tolerance and acceptance means that an identical form of sexual autonomy is classified as acceptable by one group and as inappropriate by another: such positioning diverges strong between different persons, nationalities, regions, and religions. Heteronormativity does not adhere to any clear concept, which reifies or devalues queer sexuality in any standardized way. Rather, political and cultural influencing factors call the tune—and milieu-specific components, and personal social skills are also important—in order to achieve a matching recognition for some forms of queer sexuality and genderness. Regarding particular, queer-sexual expressive forms there appears to be no alternative whatsoever apart from societal scorn. Thus, queer sexuality emerges out of desire and as a discursive construct, to which a categorical appraisal can be applied. Parallel to this, and as a concept relevant to social politics, queer sexuality becomes ever more burdened with interpretations. This development is neither surprising nor particularly recent:

> Although queer was not a popular term of self-identification at the time …, its recent deployment is often informed by those issues of identity, community and politics that she raises here. A similar scrutinising of lesbian and gay identities can be seen in the queer engagement with post-structural critiques of subjectivity and individual or collective identities, its pragmatic crystallization and deployment of recently reworked subject positions, and in its attention to the discursive formations of the various terms by which homosexuality in particular and sexuality more generally are categorised.[7]

---

7   Anna-Marie Jagose, *Queer Theory, An Introduction* (New York: New York University Press, 1996), 93.

It's only through discourse that these categorizations can gain clarity, and can only then become efficacious, when it's possible to form a common image through social interaction. Regardless of whether articulated or not, this crystallization of evaluation categories is being carried out across the board. This explains different layers of recognition for queer life in large-scale political unions, including the EU and the USA. The reality and concept of "gay territory,"[8] first identified and named decades ago, elucidates and informs us about the contemporary proximity of discrepancies in social politics. In a single region, both queer freedom, and a queer failure of understanding, can take place in the same blinking of an eye, and can unfold from these two contrasting points. Continuing to think along this vein will inevitably build a bridge to the debate on gender equality and equality of opportunity. Because although those evaluation categories and layers of recognition become particularly apparent in the case of queer genderedness and sexualities, they can in no way be reduced to the same:

> Partnerships for life, as a relationship model, distinguish themselves precisely by being different from marriage, and through an updating of the gender and sexuality hierarchies connected with the marriage model. I want again to emphasize the interwovenness of sexuality and gender, and the benefits of working with the critical concepts of heteronormativity, in not simply reducing these contexts to an isolated "discrimination on the basis of sexual orientation": it's precisely the interplay of normative heterosexuality and homophobia, which structure hierarchical gender-based relations.[9]

---

8   Robert W. Bailey, "Sexual Identity and Urban Space, Economic Structure and Political Action," in: *Sexual Identities, Queer Politics*, ed. Mark Blasius (New Jersey: Princeton University Press, 2001), 231.

9   Anna Böcker, *Weder gleich- noch que(e)rstellen. Heteronormativität, Reproduktion und Citizenship in den Debatten zur Lebenspartnerschaft*, (Berlin: Gender Politik Online, 2011), 17, https://www.fu-berlin.de/sites/gpo/pol_sys/politikfelder/Weder_gleich_noch_queerstellen/annaboeckerglecihnochqueerstellen.pdf.

Although evaluation structures encircle the readability of gender and sexuality, a *queering* becomes possible, as soon as recognized yet unarticulated criteria are not fulfilled. In so doing, sexual and gender-based disturbances flow every which way, and far beyond the areas defined by Gayle Rubin, as a range of scholarly studies have affirmed for decades. The role of women, images of ideal manliness, collective notions of beauty, and thoughts about an optimized corporeality: all these are subject to trends and transformations:

> It is beyond dispute that, broadly speaking, developments of the sort charted by Rubin[10] are happening throughout most Western societies—and to some extent in other parts of the world as well. Of course, there are significant divergences between different countries, subcultures and socio-economic strata. Certain groups, for example, stand apart from the sort of changes described, or actively attempt to resist them. Some societies have a longer history of sexual tolerance than others and the changes which they are experiencing are perhaps not quite as radical as in the US. In many, however, such transitions are happening against the backdrop of more constraining sexual values than were characteristic of American society several decades ago. For people living in these contexts, particularly women, the transformations now occurring are dramatic and shattering.[11]

This constant development of an enhancement and devaluation of sexual and bodily performances, and the becoming visible that is linked to this, is grounded in both a social-cultural tradition and in innovation. This is a game of achieving balance between a striving toward emancipation and a heteronomous tolerance/a hoped-for acceptance:

> Sexual emancipation, I think, can be the medium of a wide-ranging emotional reorganisation of social life. The concrete meaning of

---

10   Lilian Rubin is an American sociologist and psychotherapist. For more information: https://lilli anrubin.com/.

11   Anthony Giddens, *The Transformation of Intimacy, Sexuality, Love and Eroticism in Modern Societies* (Stanford: Stanford University Press, 1992), 12n.

> emancipation in this context is not, however, as the sexual radicals proposed, a substantive set of psychic qualities or forms of behaviour. It is more effectively understood in a procedural way, as the possibility of the radical democratisation of the personal. Who says sexual emancipation, in my view, says sexual democracy. It is not only sexuality at stake here. The democratisation of personal life, as a potential, extends in a fundamental way to friend ship relations and, crucially, to the relations of parents, children and other kin.[12]

This sexual democratization, which was described as such in the 1990s through the work of the British sociologist Anthony Giddens already, is formed, and made tangible for the individual, out of broad-based societal influences—including media or politics—alongside the impacts effected by family and friends. This is why a sexual emancipation of people is required, which, on Giddens' view, must be conceived of in terms of processes:

> It would be a daredevil act of understatement to say that not all gays and lesbians share this view of the new queer politics. It will continue to be debated for some time. I have made my own sympathies clear because the shape of any engagement between queer theory and other social-theoretical traditions will be determined largely by the political practice in which it comes about. In fact, however, no term—even "queer"—works equally well in all the contexts that have to be considered by what I am nevertheless calling queer theory. Queer activists are also lesbians and gays in other contexts – as for example where leverage can be gained through bourgeois propriety, or through minority-rights discourse, or through more gender-marked language (it probably won't replace lesbian feminism). Queer politics has not just replaced older modes of lesbian and gay identity; it has come to exist alongside those older modes, opening up new possibilities and problems whose relation to more familiar problems is not always clear. Queer theory, in short, has much work to do just in keeping up with queer political culture. If it contributes to the self-

---

12   Giddens, *The Transformation*, 182.

clarification of the struggles and wishes of the age, it may make the world queerer than ever.[13]

The contextualization of a queer sexuality turns up again in multidimensional settings—the natures of these are family-based, sociocultural, subcultural, media-based, political, and many others besides. In so doing, it influences one's own shame, and the kind of conscience that's been formed up until this point. Sex that's perceived as "worse," more dirty, more deficient, more banal, more chaotic, less protected, or indeed more unconventional, remains a risky decision in practice, but much more so in public avowals of the same—or in public attributions applied to it. Whoever completes a performance worthy of any of these adjectives is guilty, should experience shame, even when, or rather precisely when, such performances take place in secret, in the dark, or in private.

While queer sexuality may possess clear forms within theoretical and political frameworks, in quotidian coexistence, the boundaries have become at least partially fluid. If the new sexual and gender-based normality admits same-gender desire, and adequately assimilated forms of trans identity, this principally signifies an assumption of heteronormative game rules by those who have sufficient will power and possibilities to apply such rules. These may include two men in a relationship, with an adequate ratio of proximity to distance, who concurrently fulfill clichés arising from the particular situation; the single but self-sacrificing lesbian activist; or the trans woman who has arrived authentically in the social target gender. These are only three examples of the many opportunities, packed with chances, for a milieu-specific kind of recognition.

But, from this perspective, whoever doesn't fit into such schemes should hide, and who doesn't "function" on these terms would be well advised to persevere in silence. A visible breaking out of any particular niche of queer sexuality is sanctioned by tabooing, stigmatization, and

---

13 Michael Warner, "Introduction," in *Fear of a Queer Planet, Queer Politics and Social Theory*, ed. Michael Warner, (Minneapolis: University of Minnesota, 2004), xxviii.

anti-solidarity, if the form of queerness assumed cannot be processed by society. In these terms, it's not a queer "Being-Different" a priori that's the transgression, but rather being different in a specific expressive form, which turns out too contrary to a dominant, normed image in public performance. The repeatedly applied categorization, fluid in how it represents itself—a categorization that must perforce be understood as capricious, and milieu-specific—carries historical traditions into the future, which primarily consider conservative understandings of compulsive stability. Parallel to this, there's an apprehension of new and partially queer forms of representing sociocultural expansion politics—when assimilating makes this possible—in order to generate new waves of recognition, which can affirm or match with the foundations of the systemic canon of values:

> Thus, it seems that the crucial issue is a permanent altercation with human intimacies and their visibility, a spectacle playing out in the antechamber of recognized sexualities. In this process, publicly visible same-gender inclination threatens to injure the fragile construct of order surrounding interpersonal proximity. Visible love between two women or two men turns invisible but evident sexuality into a parade and leads to an acute lack of explanation. The compulsion grows to articulate unstated principles and more: to have to legitimate a heteronormative order that's already a given. Which encompasses not merely a sexual order, but also the norm of gender-based behavioral means. Fitting into a role as a man or a woman, and betrayal—through intimacy with one's own gender—leads unavoidably to a crisis of definition, what the norm actually is, and to a disordering of the visible. Only distance from public life, even when clarity concerning the relationship between two people is already established, supports and calms the norm and order of sexuality and gender.[14]

In terms of conforming to normative notions, this "antechamber of power"[15] provides the recognition of sexual or gender-based compo-

---

14 Martin J. Gössl, *Schöne, queere Zeiten?*, 22.
15 Gössl, 22.

nents of queerness, a recognition that achieves itself step by step, or continues itself silently. This is not about a general amnesty, but rather a dynamic of negotiation between: political demands and counter-demands; traditions; economic, media-based, and cultural influencing factors; and an international, ethical discourse. This form of debate is abstract and yet omnipresent, which is why theoretical appropriations can only represent one side of the coin. It's particularly sexuality—queer sexuality—which likes to come to the fore in practical everyday life, with all its difficulties:

> In queer theory, the cultural production of norms and normality, the exposition of the "other," and the inclusions and exclusions connected with that, have, until now, only rarely been placed in relation with the structurally constructing influence of capital valorization, exploitation, and economic compulsion no how lives are led … . We thus risk losing sight of the reason behind the reproduction of the hierarchical differences that are imposed on one another, in which the "increase" in freedom for some comes accompanied by a "decrease" in freedom for others. But self-evidently, this social (re)-differentiation is heteronormatively structured. The answer to whether this must necessarily be the case, and the consequences of this answer for critiquing heteronormativity, will determine whether [participants in] sexual politics wish to be no more than affirmative coworkers, laboring away at modernizing what already exists. Or whether sexual politics can form the bedrock of a societal project to rock the boat of societal relations.[16]

An important component of the boat of societal relations mentioned above are indeed the sanctioning mechanisms of power that push what is unacceptably queer to the peripheries of society, perception, and solidarity. Attractive collaborations, which reach into a queer subculture,

---

16 Peter Wagenknecht, "Was ist Heteronormativität? Zu Geschichte und Gehalt des Begriffs," in: *Heteronormativität, Empirische Studien zu Geschlecht, Sexualität und Macht*, ed. Jutta Hartmann, Christian Klesse, Peter Wagenknecht, Bettina Fritzsche, and Kristina Hackmann (Wiesbaden: Springer, 2007), 30.

make those logical alliances brittle that disfigure thematic connectedness and fuel segregation within queer scenes and subcultures, despite what actors know about heteronormative fickleness:

> This new persecution of the peripheral sexualities entailed an incorporation of perversions and a new specification of individuals. As defined by ancient civil or canon law, sodomy was one category [among several] forbidden acts; its perpetrator was the juridical subject of this act, but not more than this. The nineteenth-century homosexual became a personage, a past, a case history, and a childhood, in addition to being a type of life, a life form, and a morphology, with an indiscreet anatomy and a possibly mysterious physiology. Nothing that went into his total composition was unaffected by his sexuality. It was everywhere present in him everywhere: at the root of all his actions because it was their insidious and indefinitely active principle; written immodestly on his face and body because it was a secret that always gave itself away. It was consubstantial with him, less as a habitual sin than as a singular nature. ... The sodomite had been a temporary aberration; the homosexual was now a species.[17]

Judith Butler, a scholar of gender and queerness, also elaborates on this thought, in concluding that:

> Note as well that the category of sex and the naturalized institution of heterosexuality are constructs, socially instituted and socially regulated fantasies or "fetishes," not natural categories, but political ones (categories that prove that recourse to the "natural" in such contexts is always political). Hence, the body which is torn apart, the wars waged among women, are textual violences, the deconstruction of constructs

---

17   Michael Foucault, *The History of Sexuality, Volume I: An Introduction*, trans. Robert Hurley, (New York: Pantheon Books, 1978), 42–43. Note by translator of this volume, Henry Holland: I have adapted Hurley's translation. Despite all its merits, Hurley's translation muddies Foucault's intentions at certain points, rather than clarifying them.

that are always already a kind of violence against the body's possibilities.[18]

In a subsequent step, this theoretical singularity is applied by Michael Warner in an exemplary analysis of different large cities in the USA, including New York:

> The current conditions in New York vividly illustrate what happens when national and international forces push the expansion of a market at the expense of public space and public autonomy, while at the same time lesbian and gay organizations decide that privacy and normalization are their goals. Gay men and lesbians collectively are exceedingly ill equipped now to recognize or resist the shifts in public culture. The media that organize the lesbian and gay public have changed, along with the rest of the culture; they are increasingly dominated by highly capitalized lifestyle magazines, which themselves have been drawn into close partnership with the mass entertainment industry through the increased visibility of some gay celebrities and the increased use of gay-themed plots in mass culture.[19]

Does this mean some protagonists in a queer subculture are corrupt collaborators? And do a few queer segments of recognition suffice to break apart the solidarity of a community of queer sexualities and genders?

In the twenty-first century, many queer challenges remain tangible and visible, but also negotiable. The institutions and communities, which have been participating in a broad-based discourse on sexual and gender-based, have extended themselves, and in some cases positioned themselves anew. Increasingly, international perspectives are being added to political perceptions. This is why national discrepancies pertaining to queer living conditions can irritate concerned parties, thus benefiting participants' ability to participate in discourse and in action.

---

18   Judith Butler, *Gender Trouble: Feminism and the Subversion of Identity* (New York: Routledge, 2006), 172.
19   Michael Warner, *The Trouble with Normal: Sex, Politics, and the Ethics of Queer Life* (Cambridge: Harvard University Press, 1999), 162n.

This can be seen, for example, in a queer refugees' movement—i.e. the explicit emigration away from the land of one's birth, because of how life is there, experienced in individual, sexual, and gender-based terms. But it can also be seen in the political noticing of discriminatory or even life-threatening threats to queer persons in other parts of the world—for example in a media focus on parliamentary bills that threaten queer people's inviolability.

In similar fashion, the provocative question concerning collaboration must be juxtaposed with a further question: isn't accessing the "antechamber of power"[20] generally beneficial for a lasting, social politics based transformation of foundational norms pertaining to genders and forms of sexual expression? Can taking on norms and standards from societal majorities have subversive effects nonetheless, and thus create space for new forms of queer love and life? Fundamental questions arising here are based on the assumption that the recognition of some queer performances can create corresponding spaces of tolerances in queer subcultural niches. This is especially relevant to those individuals who, in the long term, are likely be denied the acceptance of majorities.

It's a similar feeling to holding out in a bus shelter in rainy weather: Some manage to get on and ride in a full bus, even when there's no seat free. If that's the case, then there will definitely be at least one place free in the shelter for that person who had been standing in the rain until now, and who was ignored toughly by those who had been staying in the dry. It remains unclear, however, who now gets to move into the dry. Or rather: the haphazard crowd in the shelter means that this process is determined subtly. Similar to the power of recognition, forms of influence—government cabinet membership, for example, corporate leadership, or many other decision-making locations—have been commandeered by a single group or majority. It's all too easy to see the responsibility that others have, the person sitting next to you in the canteen, for example, or to fix one's view on the fact that one's earned one place in historical terms. This can easily lead to a postponement of every form of

---

20 See: Martin J. Gössl, *Schöne, queere Zeiten?*, 22.

solidarity with others, and to finding a "good" justification for one's own deeds. But what encroaches particularly on the responsibility for one's own actions is the possibility of successful aspiration, the chance of getting on in life, oneself, and thus the far too understandable concentration on the true tasks in life: finally getting either into the bus shelter, or even onto the approaching bus. Even when thinking in this way, clarity often prevails concerning grievances in the power system, and about the aforementioned strategies of tabooing, stigmatization, and anti-solidarity. Yet all too willingly, people often see unfair present-day conditions as the price that must be paid for one's own well-being, and in order not to endanger one's own chances, by mentioning uncomfortable facts pertaining to specific cases. The buses continue to pass by the crossroads of one's own life, and a typical kind of character always manages to get onto one bus or another.

Thus, queer sexuality remains essentially one thing above all: queer. Or put differently: the potential of this sexuality lies not merely in the chance of recognition by heteronormative power structures, but also in the articulation and performance of alternative counter-proposals and counter-publics. That's why we should enjoy existing sympathy for partial recognition forms of queer sexuality and gender, and why solidarity with queer peripheral forms should be a lived, embodied solidarity.

7. Queer Beauty

> Homosexuality is now signified by theatrically "macho" clothing (denim, leather, and the ubiquitous key rings) rather than by feminine style drag; the new "masculine" homosexual is likely to be nonapologetic about his sexuality, self-assertive, highly consumerist and not at all revolutionary, though prepared to demonstrate for gay rights. This one might note, is far removed from the hopes of the early seventies liberationists who believed in a style that was androgynous, non-consumerist and revolutionary.[1]

Ideals of particular kinds of beauty, including queer notions of beauty, are subject to permanent flux. The Australian political scientist Dennis Altman encapsulated this neatly, concerning gay, 1970s subculture, with Gay Liberation commencing soon after Stonewall. The Revolution encouraged many queer men to wear openly clothing and other signs of symbolic strength, sexual potency, and recognizable pride. Especially in the urban centers of the US, the myth that a heroic street battle had taken place in Christopher Street in New York became a leitmotif in gay self-understanding. Detached, through anti-solidarity processes, from other queer groups in this revolutionary era, the attractiveness of gay men, which was now in the limelight, was shaped and celebrated largely autonomously. That said, the concept of beauty in question was mapped in ideal terms to an old image of masculinity, and in no way a new one.

---

1   Dennis Altman, "What Changed in the Seventies," in: *Homosexuality: Power and Politics*, ed. Gay Left Collective (London, New York: Allison & Busby, 1980), 52.

In ways that were almost grotesque, many gay men began to fit perfectly into old clichés:

> Since homosexuality is always defined in terms of effeminacy, the concept of a masculine homosexual is, in the discourses of straight society, an oxymoron. The appropriation of the masculine by the gay community serves to underline the extent of gay exclusion from the dominant. The gay man who claims to be "masculine" instantly violates that masculine identification when he expresses (gay) sexual desire. Masculinity and gay sex can never be equated, trapping the gay man in a paradoxical position: possessing the anatomical sex of a man and identifying with the masculine gender, the macho gay man is at once a part of the masculine dominant and forever excluded from it because of his sexual desires. Every attempt he makes to include himself within the discourses of masculinity leads to his violation of the whole concept of "masculinity" as he becomes a perversion of its very (heterosexual) definition.[2]

Forms of beauty are subject not only to permanent transitions, but also and concurrently to milieu-specific influences. The forms of beauty in question are categories recognized by a societal majority. Alongside generally applicable cultural forms of male and female beauty, subcultures also provide utterly original forms of alternative beauty models, or nurture modes of representation, which have public effects in varying and sometimes irritating ways. What is considered beautiful, both in aesthetic as in erotic terms, becomes unmistakably political in understandings of queer beauty. Within this framework, variations in imaginations of beauty, including gay-male dominance since the 1970s, are merely one possibility among many. Queer communities have been characterized by their ability to find expressive forms of self-staging gender and sexuality. Alongside the collective and cultural-political process of finding themselves, some of these expressive forms lay a claim to beauty. And this "beauty," as a performative factor, turns in the process into a general

---

2   Jamie Russell, *Queer Burroughs* (New York: Palgrave MacMillan, 2001), 123.

commodity, superficially available to everybody, but actually egalitarian only in a limited sense of that word:

> Ideals of beauty are now reaching all groups in society. Party to these transmissions, isolated tendencies are showing that fashion is taking on inspiration from "below," meaning that it's now having less influence on higher socioeconomic strata—exceptions to this are when designer elements inside fashion take on a subculture like hip hop or punk, thus introducing these elements into "better society."
> Here we see a democratization of imperatives to beauty, which is demonstrated by the fact that beauty standards are rapidly reaching broad sections of the population. But because everybody has become an object of composition and positioning by this stage, corporeality is also a location in which societal hierarchies are reflected to a high degree.[3]

The preponderant ideals of beauty have been subject to multifarious influences for decades. That said, the public, recognized formation that the body received is not carried out exclusively by elites. The influences on the understanding of who currently counts as beautiful are disparate, and transition rapidly. It's no surprise to discover that, here too, a queer form of beauty is to be found, which reflects both general trends and specific deliberations. What's more, queer ideals of beauty are characterized by oppositions in appearance forms, through what are seen as polarities between norms and abnorms, and through visible contrariness. The breadth of queer beauty as a perceptible language directed outward can express a political statement against the establishment, but can also approve the same. And sometimes this happens to a single individual, when several queer standpoints are presented concurrently:

> The deregulation of socioeconomic strata is juxtaposed to a stringent, internalized regimentation of personal lifestyles. This rulebook consists of many small parts, which, apparently, we choose out of

---

[3] Waltraud Posch, *Projekt Körper. Wie der Kult um die Schönheit unser Leben prägt* (Frankfurt:, Campus, 2009), 64.

> our own free will, and an ample process of selection from what seem like countless possibilities. One of these selectable small parts is the body.[4]

> The history of beauty is a history of bodies and fashions, of moral notions, stagings, power, and gender roles. And it's a history of visibility. Whichever shape ideals of beauty currently assume in any given period, that time and culture will perceive them as normality.[5]

Both the democratization of ideals of beauty, and the opportunity to perform these ideals—as a lively part of subcultural life, and/or in the virtual presentation of the same—it is differentiated images that facilitate queer patterns of beauty and their respective recognition: by a few, some, or none at all.

Although androgynous expressive forms of beauty are not new, they're more widely spread than ever before in postmodern, virtually interconnected societies. Classic, optical boundaries in the gender tradition are rendered fluid by such forms, and can be playfully reinterpreted as a provocation. This means, in any case, that aesthetics take a back seat, i.e. the fashionable interpretation of beauty in human guise, extending beyond the borders of biological femininity or masculinity. This also means that androgynous linguistic forms become a component of fashion design, youth cultures, and all kinds of subcultural expressive forms, each with the potential to exert influence within societal majorities:

> While the fashion and beauty world's adoration of androgyny has endured for decades, the latest shift isn't about women borrowing from men or vice versa, but a seemingly casual move beyond gender altogether. ... For Canadian designer Rad Hourani—whose campaigns have spotlighted lean, delicately featured guys and slighthipped, makeup-less girls for years—androgyny is all about a freeing ease. It's

---

4   Posch, *Projekt*, 66n.
5   Posch, *Projekt*, 172.

far from the aggressively theatrical school of "70s androgyny," defined by a face-painted David Bowie and company. Hourani's unisex architectural designs are boundary breakers, sure, but he also calls them "modern classics," "comfortable" and "asexual." ... In today's tech-driven age, could the new androgyny be an effort to find an aesthetic sympatico with our avatar-constructed lives? ... In a sign of the times, this year Facebook expanded its list of gender options for users from two (female, male) to 50-plus, including agender, androgyne, gender fluid, gender nonconforming, gender questioning and neutrois.[6]

This playing with gender-based and sexual interpretative patterns in fashion and clothing can represent both the zeitgeist in question, and a practical detachment from political demands since first-wave feminism. What began as claims made by individuals, including, notably, Paul O'Montis or Marlene Dietrich, has been interpreted in an increasingly broad-manner over the decades. Thus, the game of playing with androgynous appearance reveals its true colors to be an expressive form in both historical and cultural ways, whereby the strong queer threads remain evident:

> The new sexual freedom that many rock'n'roll songs championed in the 1960's, for example, was more an assertion of dissent and attitude than it was a reflection of everyday life in youth subculture. Within gay subculture, however, a flaunting of society's more was, and remains, part of daily life. This unconventional lifestyles, with the emphasis on "style," was viewed somewhat enviously by popular music's more stylish performers, who have consistently appropriated gay style and mediated that discourse of fashion for their fans. ... It is well-known, of course, that Bowie, Reed, Iggy Pop and Bryan Ferry and Brian Eno (both of Roxy Music) were all regular visitors to the most fashionable gay haunts on both sides of the Atlantic [Europe and North America]

---

6   Durga Chew-Bose, "The Androgynous Beauty Mood of the Moment, The blurred lines between feminine and masculine is a blasé bending of expectations," in: Flare on November 27, 2014, https://www.flare.com/beauty/the-androgynous-beautymood-of-the-moment/.

and that four of the five—Ferry is the exception—posed for years as bisexual and/or gay at different items.[7]

Both artists and non-conformist thinkers have not only invented themselves out of their own creativity, but have also concurrently articulated a standpoint, which has developed an important, cultural valence for some. Yet, now we've arrived in the twenty-first century, these standpoints appear to have disintegrated into fields that offer a large numbers of people alternative forms of expression, and the possibility of being beautiful. Androgynous representative forms have arrived in our everyday lives, accompanied by the fraught possibility that they might be recognized as beautiful. They function successfully amongst the media's dominant abbreviations of beauty, which continue to mold the great surface for projections on offer here, as long as an artistic valuable attribution appears possible. But as soon as this freedom of art, and, in some cases, of scholarship too, is left behind, entirely different informal rules come into play:

> "Contemporary teen film" depiction of LGBT characters generally conforms to the same hegemonically dominant "tendencies" visible in mainstream media: they tend to be white, middle-class, able-bodied; they tend to be gay, or perhaps lesbian, but rarely bisexual or transgender. Their desires tend to be chaste, insinuated more than stated, and they tend to come out and declare recognisable, binary, fixed identities, with well-adjusted, happy, healthy portrayals tending to be out and proud, and deviance related to closet-cases. And yet, these tendencies are also contested within the genre. There are—though few and far between—non-white, non- middle-class characters. There are lesbians, bisexuals, and even a very few transgender characters. While culturally understood as victims, onscreen LGBT youth often face no

---

7   B. Fergus Foley, "Significant Others: Gay Subcultural Histories and Practices," (PhD diss., Simon Fraser University, 1987), 149n.

onscreen victimisation, and those that do use their own agency to overcome adversity.[8]

Even when white skin color, physical integrity, and fitness influence how current physiognomic standards, in terms of an individual's looks, and many further factors in the media's means of representing queer persons are fulfilled, it's particularly postmodern, virtually interconnected communities that can create alternative forms of performance and images, to subculturally extend the frameworks of beauty. Critical reflections on a dominant, majority-based society and a steering toward a subcultural community are evidently necessary, to give alternatives a chance. But it's the very process of subcultural standards becoming visible, and the connected democratization of which expressive forms count as beautiful, which provided evidence for the increasing importance of queer power in definition. The tenacity and omnipresence of media make it easier to accept and to internalize currently existing standards. However, virtual possibilities also lend wings to newly gained autonomy, and the potential turn to global alternatives:

> I do not feel that I fit the traditional definitions of male and female. I am somewhere in the middle. For some reason, this scares some people. People have a hard time accepting what they cannot see or cannot relate to. Not everyone questions their gender. But there is no real rule to androgyny.[9]

Indeed, it is genuinely the lack of rules—or, expressed differently, the freedom—which unsettles people in relation to androgyny. Deprived of the anchoring points of a gender-based assignment perceptible from without, observers are left in a state of irritation, which can only be

---

8   Andrea Pauline MacRae, "Hegemonic negotiation and LGBT representation in contemporary teen films," (PhD diss., University of Western Australia, 2018), 157.
9   Jordan McGee, "Confident and Comfortable: The Beauty of Androgyny" in: *Grand Central Magazine*, February 15, 2017, http://gcmag.org/confident-and-comfortable-the-beauty-of-androgyny/.

dissipated by an attempt to make contact. Beyond that, although an androgynous appearance form eludes the scope of a general set of rules, it cannot elude aesthetic judgments. That said, while a performance of one's own personality, which cuts across barriers of gender and sex, may proceed from an idea of emancipation, the democratization of ideals concerning beauty also creates subcultural evaluation tendencies. This is because traditional, creative, or even disdainful understandings of beauty will still also prevail in subcultures and their subfields. These understandings, and their codes, identifying characteristics, and forms of expression, continue to exert influence:

> Gay men have long experimented with notions of acceptability in behaviour and dress. The twentieth century has seen a movement in the (straight) public's perceptions of gay men and also in the positioning of gay men's self-identity. Codes of behaviour and styles of presentation that were utilised by gay men have developed and been cast aside as social attitudes and legal positions have altered. Stereotypes that were formed have been challenged, broken down and replaced by new ones. ... there has been a breakdown of the gay and non-gay "us and them," fashion and dress choice are still used by many to differentiate themselves, sometimes as individuals, sometimes as members of a group and sometimes as both.
> Many gay men no longer feel the need to define their identity through their choice of dress, while others are making conscious efforts to reinforce a communal identity through behaviour and locations for living and working and dress. One fact that does remain is gay men's interest in clothing; but even that is no longer homogenous ... .[10]

The polymath and semiotician Umberto Eco nailed this development squarely, in his book on the history of beauty, and its historical and aesthetic dimensions:

---

10   Shaun Cole, *"Don We Now Our Gay Apparel": Gay Men's Dress in the Twentieth Century* (Oxford: Berg, 2000), 189.

For their part, the mass media no longer present any unified model, any single ideal of Beauty. They can retrieve, even for an advertising campaign destined to last only a week, all the experimental work of the avant-garde, and at the same time offer models from the 1920s, 1930s, 1940s and 1950s, even in the outmoded forms of automobiles from the mid-century. The mass media continue to serve up warmed-over versions of nineteenth-century iconography, the Junoesque opulence of Mae West and the anorexic charms of the latest fashion models; the dusky Beauty of Naomi Campbell and the Nordic Beauty of Claudia Schiffer; the grace of traditional tap dancing as in A Chorus Line and the chilling futuristic architectures of Blade Runner, the femme fatale of dozens of television shows or advertising campaigns and squeaky-clean girls-next-door like Julia Roberts or Cameron Diaz; Rambo and RuPaul; George Clooney with his short hair, and neo-cyborgs who paint their faces in metallic shades and transform their hair into forests of coloured spikes, or shave their heads.

Our explorer from the future will no longer be able to identify the aesthetic ideal diffused by the mass media of the twentieth century and beyond. He will have to surrender before the orgy of tolerance, the total syncretism and the absolute and unstoppable polytheism of Beauty.[11]

Following Eco's conclusions, will queer beauty soon be unchained and ready to become even more compartmentalized? Are social attributions and societal limitations on the edge of disbanding, as soon as one has arrived in the right sub-community? The democratization of queer forms concerning ideals of beauty and alternatives has become more visible, but obstinate currents of exclusion and inclusion remain nonetheless. Particularly virtual meeting and dating platforms display, in their reductive focus on visual, specific, and broad-based forms of marginalization, and the application of homogeneous ideals of beauty. The representation of one's self through images and only a few words reduces human beings to the merely obligatory; depending on the

---

11   Umberto Eco, *On Beauty: A History of a Western Idea*, ed. Umberto Eco, trans. Alastair McEwen, (London: Seeker & Warburg, 2004), 426-428.

platform, this could be relationship forms, sexuality, and/or sexual preferences. The construction of this kind of apps for cellphones mostly makes this reduction clear, through the design and the functions offered. At the same time, the popularity of these apps proves not only their widespread reach, but also how they've established themselves successfully in postmodern, virtually interconnected societies. Regardless of whether self-description or search functions pre-state ethnic or indeed physical characteristics for selection, it takes only seconds for individual visual judgment schemes to take hold, powered by internalized patterns of social recognition and slumbering ideals of beauty. A single attentive swipe suffices to take a decision, the snippets of information presented being skimmed read, again, in seconds, and scoured for predetermined breaking points. Cultural codes, verifiable educational qualifications, a person's job or even their income can all be identified accurately using familiar symbols—when people use these to deceive deliberately, this already problematic practice becomes even worse. And, assuming users even want to know or communicate this stuff, positions on ideological affiliations and spiritual attitudes to life can be relayed. These abbreviations of one's own identity becomes a billboard, adorned with a typical, presentable smile, whereby some users still shy away intensive us e of image optimizing programs. The exaggeration of advantageous facets is intended to foreground what is presented as self-evident, so that users can offer whichever attributes are considered desirable this month: super slim, super-athletic, super-popular, super-rich and super-beautiful:

> They'll claim statements like "no fats," "no fems," "no asians," and "no blacks" are nothing more than preferences which they can't be blamed for, despite the fact that dating, attraction, and desire are and have always been political. ... People use the word "preference" when they don't really know what it means. The big question is, since when

is it okay to judge an entire group of people before you meet them? They've got a word for that: prejudice.[12]

This boiling complexity down to just a few—mostly visible—parameters do little more than fuel old clichés. Focusing too narrowly on beauty ideals is often misjudged, and interpreted positively, as clarity about one's own desires, especially when generalized exclusions of entire groups of people are executed in the process. Exposing this so-called clarity brings to light strategies to exclude people from the spectrum of attractiveness based on external, social and cultural markers. These prejudices and attributions are forced onto several groups, in order to optimize, in the eyes of those clicking these options, the action radius of their desire. Knowing what one finds beautiful in the queer community often seems inseparable with greater awareness of what can be understood as unattractive or even ugly:

> Those Asian men who are featured as desirable in the gay media are those who have been able to "successfully" assimilate to the dominant Anglo gay culture (e.g., Anglo features, muscular, gay fashions) … Men from Southeast Asian backgrounds in this study were frequently highly sensitive to their subordinate positioning in the dominant gay culture, in ways that Anglos would have had difficulty even noticing. For instance, in addition to being absent in the media, their experiences of being "invisible" to other participants on the scene, such as being ignored by bar staff and catching disapproving glances from Anglo and other European patrons … .[13]

The mechanisms that kick in on digital platforms are hardly new, but rather virtual continuations: the daily marginalization of a supposed

---

12 Buffy Flores, "This 'No Fats, No Fems' Shirt Is Everything That's Wrong With the Gay Community," *Pride* on April 28, 2016, https://www.pride.com/firstperson/2016/4/28/no-fats-no-fems-shirt-everything-thats-wrong-gay-community.

13 Damien Ridge, Amos Hee, and Victor Minichiello, "Asian Men on the Scene," in: *Journal of Homosexuality* 36, no. 3–4 (1999), 47, https://www.tandfonline.com/doi/abs/10.1300/J082v36n03_03.

Other, ad infinitum. The building of hierarchical systems, the forms in which they're applied, and their heedless but apparently expedient use, all utilize well-known labelling and stigmatization strategies: and these are grounded in socially constructed—and queer—beauty formulas:

> It is also interesting to note that while ten ethnic labels are offered by Grindr, these categories are centred on western civilisations, offering labels for major groups such as "White" and "Black," as well as subcontinental groups such as "Native American" and "Latino." Middle Eastern ethnicity are represented by "Middle Eastern," while Asia is represented by "Asian" and "South Asian," despite being the largest, most ethnically diverse and populous continent. All other individuals are simply accounted for in "Other." In contrast, we see more general options offered by Jack'd[14]–"Asian," "Black," "Caucasian," "Latino," "Middle Eastern," "Mixed," "Pacific Islander" and "Other." As many interviewees expressed, underrepresentation of accurate ethnicities and/or cultural identities result in the selection of "Blank," "Prefer not to say" or other equivalent options offered. While ethnic filtering may facilitate prejudice against certain ethnic groups, many users describe these exclusions as non-racially motivated and simply a matter of personal taste. Researchers have argued that tastes and interested of individuals are ultimately shaped through socio-economic, as well as locational factors, and not necessarily a matter of taste, but an issue relating to cultural and political differences ... .[15]

As unifying as queerness may appear, because of shared "transgressions" in the eyes of mainstream society, and because of subcultural intersections, the cracks of heteronormativity can still be found, nonetheless, in the antechamber of power's exterior facade.[16] Increasingly, the innovative power of queer beauty is gaining visibility and recognition, but much

---

14   Jack'd is an app-based chat and dating platform for a queer public: https://www.jackd.com/.
15   Wei-Hong Tseng, "'NO ASIANS PLEASE,' 'ONLY FOR ASIANS': Experiences of East-Asian Gay Newcomers on Grindr and Jack'd in London," (PhD diss., Goldsmiths University of London, 2017), 50n.
16   See: Martin J. Gössl, *Schöne, queere Zeiten?*, 22.

everyday culture is enduringly chained to old traditions of masculinity and femininity. Even when viscous streams of change of change begin to flow, and are celebrated frantically by some as emancipation from old patterns, they not only flow slowly, but are also always dangerous, as progress could turn out simply to be a new form of regression. Utterly apolitically and inconspicuous, beauty patterns serve as a roadworthy vehicle in these outpourings, which shape both lifestyles and ideological standpoints. The experience of attractiveness, the approximation to standards of contemporary beauty, and the desire for flawlessness all impact actors' behavior, subtly but substantially, in both holistic and subcultural ways.

Queer creativity, conceptualized as the power to arrive at new ideas for forms of beauty, offers both the revolutionary potential to defy established traditions, and aids normative processes of efficacy. Thus, queerness inherent in beauty leaves room for alternative interpretations of its appearance forms, and provides freedom in desire and creativity for the interpretation of attractiveness. It limits itself to neither old traditions nor perceptible facets, but allows discovery, which should be cognized in personal terms, but also collectively, and with reference to the real and the virtual. This freedom may seem exhausting for many, as it disposes of comfortable forms of beauty concepts—which ideally also include certain forms of recognition. Shedding the imaginary checklists of what makes people and things more beautiful, and what we should better give a miss, inevitably impacts back onto one's own appearance. With the result that perceived and experienced concepts of beauty must now be critically scrutinized and adapted. Although they go hand in hand with this new thinking, neither aesthetics nor desire are up for negotiation—both are allowed to, and indeed must continue to have a personal rightness, as a sensibility. However, the social automatisms of exclusion based on preconceived notions of beauty should now be recognized as what they are: labels, stigma, and prejudices.

8. Queer Cultures

Since identity is the product of a relation of power, queer identity and queer culture must necessarily change as the unacceptable becomes acceptable, however transitory that acceptability might be.[1]

Thomas Peele, an American literary and cultural studies scholar, cuts to the essential chase of queer cultures with this remark in his introduction to a twenty-first century anthology on the subject. When identities and their subcultures are created, shaped, favored, or hindered by powerful discourses, building on Peele's view, then new understanding of queer culture must be based on critiquing these very discourses. In this fashion, queer and non-queer understandings of culture by no means unfold to become unconnected antitheses, but should rather become critical juxtapositions of established scenes and performances. These cultural interactions rely on each other, and are in a constant and productive exchange. Nothing has a more disinhibiting effect than queer cultural transgression and exaggeration of normative boundaries. That said, there are few activities that create such general applause as the imitation and interpretation of queer identities. Whether these are popular or intellectually imposed cultural creations, the analogies to the world of others can only function by playing with creative assumptions and clichés:

---

1   Thomas Peele, "Introduction: Popular Culture, Queer Culture," in: *Queer Popular Culture, Literature, Media, Film, and Television*, ed. Thomas Peele, (New York: Springer, 2007), 7.

> *Will & Grace*[2] makes homosexuality safe for broadcast television audiences by framing its characters within the familiar popular culture convention that equates gayness with a lack of masculinity and through the familiar situation comedy genre conventions of romantic comedy and delayed consummation, infantilization, and an emphasis on characters' interpersonal relationships rather than the characters' connections to the larger social world. Taken together, these conventions work to confine homosexuality within its paradoxical position in dominant heteronormative discourses; homosexuality can only be represented through heterosexist categories and language, while at the same time it is marked as a deviation from the norm.[3]

Thus, queer cultural forms are not merely multifarious in their subcultural self-image, but are also multidimensional in the interpretations of social majorities deployed. Over and above media manifestations, it is foremost behaviors, oral language habits, and cultural codes—ranging across popular idols, geographical locations, fashionable analogies, bar and theater cultures, and visible lifestyles—that can undergo interpretative exegesis. These expressive forms bring same-gender desire and gender diversity into the public sphere, so they can be thought about together—in queer or non-queer circles—as ideas. Gender and sex play immanent roles in these processes—for example in language codes or symbols—both as points of departure for what is held in common, and in the experience of desire and competition. Such ambiguities are particularly remarkable in queer jokes, in which quickly going on the verbal offense, combined with being able to give as good as you get, is what can secure dominance in group dynamic terms. People enjoy demanding this ability of drag queens, whereby the targets of attacks can be anyone either inside or out with their own community. The popular drag

---

2   See: *Will & Grace*, TV series produced in the USA, 1998–2020), https://www.imdb.com/title/tt0157246/.
3   Kathleen Battles and Wendy Hilton-Morrow, "Gay Characters in Conventional Spaces: Will and Grace and the Situation Comedy Genre," *Critical Studies in Media Communication* 19, no. 1 (2002), 101n., https://doi.org/10.108 0/07393180216553.

queen Alaska Thunderfuck[4] understands herself especially concerning the scathing humor expected of her, as a reflective shaman:

> Well, because ultimately drag queens are truth-tellers. My best friend Jeremey's philosophy is that drag queens are modern-day shamans. ... They go through a transformation. There's a lot of tradition and culture that goes into that. Then, on stage, they have an ability to reflect back at you your truth and truths about society we don't want to think about. So ultimately, everything is fake: the hair, the body, the fingernails—but in that fakeness something real is able to be exposed. That isn't why I got into drag. I got into drag because it was cool. But learning about why drag was cool is something that I love that came later.[5]

Indeed, when a cultural form is trivialized, participants also gain the freedom to deliberately irritate and provoke. The ridicule thrown at drag queens doesn't only come from people who follow heteronormative norms, but also, at least occasionally, by participants in queer communities. The provocation inherent in drag art, namely transgressing gender attributions, is only the most visible level of irritation, although there's no doubt that this, in itself, irritates both inside and out with the queer community. The provocation is often intensified when ideals of beauty, behavior and several other major issues become the target of attack. Even though, through queer history, most drag artists couldn't gain access to the biggest stages, a virtue was made out of this necessity, with almost any space up for grabs as a potential stage for an amusing performance. And during all these interventions and altercations, queer perspectives on sexuality and gender always remained the starting point for interpreting the existing world: with all its shady and sunny sides. It is precisely out of this understanding that drag can be seen as an essen-

---

4   See: Alaska Thunderfuck, https://alaskathunderfuck.com/.
5   David Reddish, "Are drag queens modern-day shamans? Alaska takes us to the church of drag comedy" in: *Queerty* on April 24, 2021, https://www.queerty.com/drag-queens-modern-day-shamans-alaska-takes-us-church-drag-comedy-20210414.

tial, queer community art form, in which oppression and persecution, as well as laughing at oneself, are commemorated and celebrated.

Moreover, interested observers have diagnosed three parameters in queer cultures that have been and continue to be profoundly influential in postmodern, virtually interconnected societies. These cultural characteristics include *physical vitality, a perpetual party-mood, and essential indestructibility*:

> Last month the Centers for Disease Control and Prevention released a report concluding that gay, lesbian and bisexual people in the United States had higher rates of self-reported underlying conditions like cancer, heart disease and obesity than heterosexual people and are also more likely to be smokers. These conditions put adults at increased risk for severe illness from Covid-19, the report said.[6]

Physical vitality can be understood as both in-your-face advertising for sexual desire, and as a social vehicle, whose fundamental function is participation in queer social and cultural life. This vitality is a principle and foundational moment, which many enjoy drawing on as a precondition for being able to take part completely. It forms the basis on which elements of subcultural socialization are built upon:

> Our study found that alcohol played a key role in identity construction for LGBT people in Scotland. Respondents described the necessity of consuming alcohol to gain courage to first access the gay scene, the expectation that heavy drinking would continue to form an integral part of "nights out" on the gay scene, and persistent peer pressure to drink across the life-course. The conventional binary opposition (pints of beer signify "masculinity," sweet colourful cocktails and alcopops signify "femininity") was reversed to signify non-heteronormativity (i.e. lesbians drink pinks of beer while gay men drink cocktails and

---

6   Christina Caron, "L.G.B.T.Q. People Face Increased Risks From Covid, but Many Don't Want the Vaccine" in: *New York Times, May 5,* 2021, https://www.ny ti mes.com/2021/03/05/well/lgbtq-covid-19-vaccine.html?referringSource=arti-cleShare.

alcopops). Even when respondents rejected these stereotypes, there was a sense that these powerful associations still influenced people's drinking practices.[7]

The primary purposes served by the queer cultural understanding of physical vitality are acting as a social entity, and carrying out queer collective performances—or to be able to attend them without almost any physical restrictions. This includes a physical framework for action offering participative opportunities. On top of this, specific physical actions are involved—which we could call rituals—that make it possible to be there in the first place. Visible cracks in these supposedly shared ideals generate a collective sense of unease, when an individual's physical condition imposes limits on standardized participations for example, or when ubiquitous actions, such as alcohol consumption, become genuine problems for certain participants. Physical and mental limitations are often swept under the carpet and declared a private matter: not only do they seem to cause collective anxiety, there's also no sense that they fit into the party culture of queer social life. Likewise, alcohol as a (sub)cultural lubricant in the queer community is only reluctantly admitted, as in society as a whole, to be a problematic addictive substance when consumed in large quantities. Cultural participation demands physical vitality, or at the very least the ability to take part without causing great annoyance to those around you. Having fun with alcohol, but decoupled from addiction; chronic illness without pain; the person in a wheelchair with an inspirational smile: these stereotypical images are allowed to represent only those challenges that can be overcome—and only then is participation welcome:

> Invisibility within both communities. LGBT people with disabilities often report that it is challenging to have their identities fully recognized. In spaces focused on disability, their unique experiences as

---

7   Carol Emslie, Jemma Lennox, and Lana Ireland, "The role of alcohol in identity construction among LGBT people: a qualitative study," in: *Sociology of Health & Illness* 39, no. 8 (2017), 1475, https://pubmed.ncbi.nlm.nih.gov/28833 252/.

> LGBT people may not be recognized. And in LGBT spaces, services and facilities may not be inclusive or accessible, including having accessible buildings or restrooms, ASL interpretation and/or CART captioning for deaf or hard of hearing people, and more.[8]

This ceaseless and merciless utilization of one's own vitality takes its toll, which also strengthens the ambiguous connection between a vital participative capability, and queer-cultural creativity:

> Research on disability has identified both nonmodifiable risk factors such as age, gender, and genetics, and modifiable risk factors such as age-related diseases, impairments, functional limitations, poor coping strategies, sedentary lifestyles, and other risk behaviors in addition to social and environmental obstacles. It is important to recognize that some of the covariates of disability in these communities are related to modifiable health behaviors, including smoking among all the groups as well as weight control among lesbians. Understanding the mechanisms through which LGB adults have an increased risk of disability is important in developing and targeting prevention efforts tailored to the specific risks they face.[9]

This deep-seated anchoring of the consumption of harmful substances, the merciless subjugation of the body, and the strong outward focus on visible vitality promote a body-hostile culture that allows little queer scope for alternatives, or chooses to push the same into organizational frameworks. In queer community groups and centers, meet-ups based on solving problems regularly constitute a fixed program component: abstinence strategies, exchange formats for so-called marginalized groups, social interactions for people with disabilities and much more.

---

8   MAP, *Movement Advancement Project: LGBT People with Disabilities*, https://www.lgbtmap.org/file/LGBT-People-With-Disabilities.pdf, 3.
9   Karen I. Fredriksen-Goldsen, Hyun-Jun Kim, and Susan E. Barkan, "Disability Among Lesbian, Gay, and Bisexual Adults: Disparities in Prevalence and Risk," in: *American Journal of Public Health* 102, no. 1 (2012), E19, https://www.ncbi.nlm.nih.gov/pmc/articles/PMC3490559/.

The need for such provision, specifically for queer audiences, is often presented as the preserve of self-advocacy groups, and is rarely experienced visibly in queer nightlife culture. Bridging the gap between vitality and a healthy lifestyle seems necessary: if the obsessive association of vitality with eternal youth and idealized body shapes can be got rid of, this has a chance to succeed.

Notions of a *perpetual party-mood* not only affect external perceptions of the queer community, but is also often based on queer subcultural self-images. Christopher Street Days and other formats have evolved in postmodern, virtually interconnected societies, steadily transforming themselves from being public protest rallies to celebratory events, whereby the contents that matter seem to have gotten lost—at least for some participants:

> Going to Gay Pride, he said, has become a "cool thing" to attend rather than a place to uplift marginalized voices and to acknowledge the community's struggle to achieve progress. He said Pride, like St. Patrick's Day or Cinco de Mayo, has been taken over by people who want an excuse to drink and party, displacing the LGBTQ community from a festival meant to celebrate it.[10]

Riotous partying certainly has been an inherent part of queer protest since shortly after the Stonewall Riots at the latest. The sheer fact that it was only possible to gain lived experience of queer partying under difficult or illegal circumstances turned putting together entertaining evenings into an important form of self-advocacy during the post-Stonewall movement:[11]

---

10   Alia Wong, "Gay Pride parades used to mean protests. Now they're an excuse for straight kids to party" in: *USA Today* on June 4, 2019, https://www.usatoday.com/story/news/LGBT-issues/2018/06/22/pride-parades-excuse-straight-kids-party/712068002/.

11   See: Martin J. Gössl, *Als die erste Münze flog und die Revolution begann. Die Homosexuellen-Bewegung in der zweiten Hälfte des 20. Jahrhunderts in den Vereinigten Staaten von Amerika* (Graz: Rosalila PantherInnen, 2009).

> One of the greatest strengths of the gay rights movement has been its ability to combine activism with fun. However, as my research shows, unless there's an intent to prioritize political agendas, group solidarity can easily be eroded. Sanker has noted that as his events have become more profitable, they've faced less opposition from public officials and conservative groups. But this profitability has meant scrubbing controversial political messages from the events to make them as palatable to as many customers as possible. Something, clearly, has been lost. Sociologists are keen to note how cultures–along with subcultures–often emerge as a way to alleviate feelings of isolation and suffering. However, cultural events often become co-opted by profit motives. When this happens, they become less about caring for one another, building a sense of community or celebrating the positive aspects of humanity.[12]

Alongside nostalgia for the good old days, the revolutionary celebratory mood of queer culture has evidently transformed itself over time, both in terms of settings and audiences. Popular events in the queer scene are becoming increasingly attractive for major sponsors, and are often attended by non-queer people. The images conveyed to the outside world are—as is necessarily the case with images—abridgements of reality: content and contexts are lost, or can only be partially depicted. In consequence, media representations, and personal memories, are relentlessly reduced to the ongoing party atmosphere of the queer scene. No matter how strongly a post-Stonewall tradition may claim the element of celebratory escape from oppressive regimes, achieving a balance, or at least some kind of working compromise, between partying and politics remains a vexed question. This is why the arguments referred to in the above by sociologist Christopher T. Connor are all too apt: particularly when his queer-historical analysis of protest and celebration is linked to the subcultural tradition of a recent past, and especially given the fact

---

12 Christopher T. Connor, "How the gay party scene short-circuited and became a moneymaking bonanza," in: *The Conversation* on February 12, 2021, https://theconversation.com/how-the-gay-party-scene-short-circuited-and-became-a-moneymaking-bonanza-153424.

that this element has been readily and intensively promoted for decades. But the successes of key or center queer demands in recent decades have been pushing other political, controversial, and necessary articulations into the margins. This trade-off has been done for profit, or to achieve broad-based—and perhaps spurious—solidarity in the background. In real and worse-case scenarios, some of these most controversial articulations have been softened by this societal negotiating process, or allowed to disappear altogether.

Yet it's evidently too early to wallow in the nostalgia of a brotherly, 1970s variety of queerness: the tried and trusted concept of political partying has always had its limits for some groups. In a written riposte to that period, the activist Sylvia Rivera penned the following critique:

> This was at pride. It was the year Bette Midler came to sing "Happy Birthday" [1973, Washington Square Park, New York City] for us. It was happy for the mainstream community, but it was not happy for us. They tried to stop drag queen entertainers from performing. It was angry because I had been scheduled for many months to speak at that rally. So I'm stubborn, and I wasn't going to have it. Because for four years we were the vanguard of the gay movement, and all of a sudden it was being taken away. We were being pushed out of something we helped create. I remember this man telling me, a straight man who was my boss at the time, when I was working in Jersey—he said, "Ray, the oppressed becomes the oppressor. Be careful. Watch it." And I saw it. And I still see it. I literally had to fight my way up onto that stage. I was beat. I got to speak. I said my piece. And I basically left the movement for many years. I didn't come back into view until the 20th anniversary.[13]

The unceasing celebratory mood is not merely put under pressure by perpetually current commercializing threats, but is also impacted long-term by queer subculture's far-reaching diversity, in which many people want to meet and exchange ideas, while others want to dedicate

---

13   Ehn Nothing, *Street Transvestite Action Revolutionaries: Survival, Revolt, and Queer Antagonist Struggle*, 53.

the center of the movement entirely to political demands. A demand's heartfelt articulation, and lively protests against social injustices are counterbalanced by the longings many have to experience at least illusory normality in the queer community, if only for brief periods. A party evening, a protest march, or an action day continues to be encumbered by the baggage of many needs, and only a few of these can be given sufficient queer recognition. But here, too, the movement's often criticized ambivalence turns out to be, in fact, something more like a fruitful symbiosis. Ultimately the most counterproductive form that one's own disempowerment can take is disinterest and a lack of participation. This absence of participation has caused at least a few of the forms taken previously by the perpetual party mood to disappear:

> In the run-up to the press conference, however, the board of the charitable association "Life+" released a statement about the charity event stopping for good. "Everyone thought the Life Ball was a ship that couldn't sink"—as members commented regarding the difficult financial situation. "This wasn't a [one-off] decision, but rather a development. A development that began in 2016, the year in which the Life Ball took a break," explained the association, before describing the debilitating period, in terms of energies, that then followed. "Financial reserves [got lost], because we spent lots of project, ring-fenced funding none the less, using up a large amount of our savings in the process, and personnel reserves [evaporated], because important and experienced staff left the association." Moreover, in the intervening period, some of our sponsors gone looking for new areas to be active in. "Resultingly, the Life Balls in 2017 and 2018 were strenuous efforts," according to the association.[14]

The Life Ball, one of the best-known event formats worldwide informed by queer philosophy, is only one event from many, which were not granted the wherewithal to survive financially. It also shows that the

---

14   APA/Red. "Ende des Life Balls: Das sind die wahren Gründe für das Aus," on May 20, 2019: https://www.vienna.at/ende-des-life-balls-das-sind-die-wahren-gruende-fuer-das-aus/6214286.

margin between broad financial support and queer recognition is a thin one.

The purported fact of *essential indestructibility* is grounded in a long, queer history of suffering. Disparate forms of queer interactions had to be discovered over the course of centuries, and still must be discovered in many localities on this earth, to facilitate lives and experiences that were alternative existences to heteronormativity. In the throes of these discoveries, localities, spaces, and niches were queered, both socially and culturally. Most of this happened in the shadow of sexual and gender-based *normality*. In this, same-gender desire represented just a single fact among many possibilities, which is why retelling the history of these subcultural realities using definitions from today is a thoroughly difficult undertaking. We can see the crystallization of divergent queer cultural forms as bound to real or virtual localities; but we can also see this formation as dependent on a particular community, which has dedicated itself to this specific cultural performance. Both routes are subject to permanent transformations, as are the real spaces in question:

> [C]ulture clashes are playing out across the nation in historically gay districts, nicknamed gayborhoods. Places like Greenwich Village in Manhattan and the Castro district in San Francisco, once incubators for the gay rights movement, have "straightened" in recent decades, leading to incidents of resistance and some angst about the effects on the L.G.B.T.Q. community.[15]

It's especially the loss of spaces that is often connected with queer people's anxiety about losing parts of their own culture. Queer culture is attributed as being immanent and essential to particular localities, and the communities living there. Many see the so-called gayborhood, i.e. queer neighborhoods, as threatened cultural spaces of urban life.

But as if this wasn't enough, the dangers circling around a queer culture clinging to the idea of indestructibility also impact each invested

---

15   Scott James, "There Goes the Gayborhood" in: *New York Times* on June 21, 2021, https://www.nytimes.com/2017/06/21/us/gay-pride-lgbtq-gayborhood.html.

individual, as the theater studies scholar Sky Gilbert concludes in his answer to the provocative and rhetorical question: "Depression, suicide and epidemic drug use? How can this be? Aren't gay men happy hedonists and rich as hell to boot?":[16]

> If the plight of gay men is so dire, why are gay magazines obsessed with pets who travel—and RuPaul? Why is the message of this year's Pride that gay men are just the same as anyone else—including, tragically, the victims of serial killers? Why are gay men dedicated to perpetrating a false image of themselves as not being victims of oppression? I believe gay men are presently passing through a kind of Stockholm Syndrome in which the captured begin to identify with their captors to such an extent that they wish to become them. In this case, it is the oppressed identifying with their oppressors.[17]

Can it be possible that queer communities are losing not only their local strongholds, but also a realistic perspective on the lively culture of oppression? Indeed, on a number of essential points, queer life does appear to be indestructible. Regardless of whether it's through laws, reforms, persecutions or escalations that a homogeneous norm wishes to establish itself, a queer culture remains standing, in a similar way that there's no way to effectively forbid desire. The expressive forms of queer culture remain equally constant, its spaces and codes, its trends and idealizations. The indestructible moment can be stopped by neither historical relicts or moralistic borders. Revolutionary theses suddenly come up face to face against the anti-theses that have long been fought for, to establish, ultimately, a new synthesis in subcultural everyday life; we should also consider the concept of marriage in these deliberations:

> The multiple, queer-theoretical strands in the debate on same-sex marriage can be systematized as follows. What's foregrounded is a

---

16   Sky Gilbert, "Is queer culture losing its radical roots?" *The Conversation*, June 19, 2018, https://theconversation.com/is-queer-culture-losing-its-radical-roots-97837.
17   Gilbert, "Is queer culture."

critique of the normative utilization and historical continued application of [the concepts] of sex, sexuality, and identity, in the support for same-sex marriage, and the draft law [accompanying it]. One such discrepancy identified in the same-sex draft law is the substantial silence concerning the significance of traditional marriage for the state's regulation of societal and sex / gender relations. This means that the demands for same-sex marriage are characterized by a decoupling of the critique of existing sexual relations in society from the feminist critique of hegemonic gender relations. Same-sex marriage is pilloried fundamentally, as being less about creating equality for homosexuality, and more about a particular form of life.[18]

Even the culture of queer relation forms, and the ideals deduced from that, changed for good in recent decades. The individual, the concepts of relations, spaces, localities, and much more all exhibit constant transformations. This shows that indestructibility certainly should not be confused with immutability. Moreover: whatever queer essence is cannot be attributed to a single expressive form, but rather invents itself, again and again, in the fact of change. Essential indestructibility is due to queer immanence, consisting of gender-based and sexual diversity, which is capable of escaping from a heteronormative framework. The inherent quality of indestructibility lies in its flexibility, a result of the pressure its experienced through any number of changes.

Queer cultures continue to develop: this was always the case and will remain so. Some ideas are carried on into the future while others fall forgotten by the wayside. The visible debates pertaining to a queer subculture reflect these natural processes—and provide theses and antitheses, before a synthesis appear—when generations begin to define themselves as such, and begin to prefer that which they long since have possessed as opposed to what is merely disdainfully present, or prefer present possessions against what has already been rejected. Vice versa, while what is old may ignite a widespread feeling of disinterest, this could lead to important lessons of a collective past—strategies in societal politics, foun-

---

18 Heike Raab, "Sexual Politics, juridische Emanzipationsdiskurse und Staat," (PhD. diss., University of Vienna, 2009), 198.

dational arguments, and more—getting lost. Thus what remains is the essential indestructibility of queer subcultures in their steadfast further development, in which new spaces and new forms of community can be experienced, despite the fact that none of this can claim the status of eternal validity.

Queer culture that is constituted out of *physical vitality, a perpetual party mood, and essential indestructibility* mold a communities collective bodies. These function as the best possible fits, which can't be applied everywhere in a surefire way, but are nonetheless popular ideas, which can be applied in a queer construction plan for a community corpus.

The culture of same-gender desire, of sexual *disorder*, of multifariousness in sex and gender, and of relationship forms with different concepts behind them, has always been a culture of the everyday, which can be found both at the level of the individual, but also at the level of the collective. Whether we're talking about hotel rooms that can be booked by the hour, which celebrate a culture of silence, or the one-off bar in Park Slope, where lesbian women have met to politicize for decades,[19] queer culture is many-sided, and changing. Some traditions can be traced back to the period of heteronormative repression, or to the proud era of Gay Liberation. Other cultural expressions can be accounted for in terms of instincts, and can thus be attributed to what is secret and hidden. Regardless how, queer culture is also always an expression of community occurrences, which follows on in the wake of creativity. It's thus hardly surprising that both invisible and visible forms of creative encounter determine queer subcultures—and occasionally even extend on into societal majorities.

It's a given that there's no accounting for taste, and it's equally true that an attempt to hierarchize all the different facets of queer everyday culture: each fragment is special in itself. The many decades since the Stonewall Revolution have not only made queer culture legally experienceable, in all its rich diversity, but have also created the possibility of

---

19 Ginger's, 363 5th Ave, Brooklyn, NY 11215, USA: https://www.lesbianbarproject.com/gingers.

nurturing and encouraging all kinds of encounter, and even of argument. This determines not only a conventional further development, which would have been foreseeable even centuries before, but also opens up other dimensions, including, for example, an open, queer youth culture, or a queer business culture. LGBTIQ people now have legal freedom in many societies in this world, in some cases a freedom that's protected from discrimination, but also the freedom to discover themselves, as both individuals and groups, and to nurture social-cultural interactions. It is possible to go forth with the unifying bond, of living alternative ideas of gender and sexuality. This move outwards into a more general public includes harnessing the perspectives thus connected with one's own cultural power to create. Out of this result, ultimately, idols, forms of humor, codes for being with one another, and much more, which can finally facilitate what we shall call queer normality.

Queer-cultural recognition is what determines the duty to assume this inheritance of one's own, community past, the care for current forms of expression attached to it, and the demands for further development. This is not merely a commission for a single community, but just as much a necessary political demand to the whole of society. Being mindful in relation to the subcultural past lends that which is queer not only forms and faces, but also perspectives for the present and the future. In so doing, one neither has to perform for a pink temple, nor revere any lilac-colored relics. Rather, this is about appreciating a multitude of queer cultural forms and their recognition as equally valuable elements of a collective identity. Beyond this, the issue is the conservation and reflective working through of these fragments—the totality of queer subcultures cannot be housed entirely in any one place—by institutions, e.g. archives, and academic professions, including chairs for research and teaching at universities. The recognition of a culture can be reconstructed precisely through its theoretical confrontations: the discursive ability, pertaining to a community of education, to articulate queer questions, and to augment the same with grounded revisions. This makes Queer Studies an immanent component of a queer culture and a queer community. Not only do they bring up facts that are defined as relevant, generating new knowledge in this field, but also conserve and interpret these facts for potential use in fact-based debates. Such structuring frameworks are determined by decisions in societal politics, which also determine what should be considered relevant, and which artefacts should be ignored—for the time being, at least. While this kind of cultural evaluation may seem reasonable within the realm of dominant heteronormativity, it's quite possible that the same will be viewed as insufficient when seen from queer perspectives, or even seen as colonialist. The queer standpoint for cultural consciousness demands visible protest. Non-existent but necessary budgets, the intentional trivialization of cultural questions, and social marginalization are all strategies regularly deployed to push queer culture into the periphery of public visibility. To accept this would simply be a further concession, an agreeing to take our seat in the "antechamber of power,"[20] without being able to co-shape relevant structures. Queer culture is the expression of a past consisting of persecution, repression, revolution, and emancipation; the same culture provides a home for everyday practices, and provides freedoms for the building of identities. It gifts us space for protests, for inclinations and for sexualities, and unchains the genders and the sexes for a plurality of potential chances for alternative normalities. All this contains merit and should be recognized for that which it is: cultural abundance.

---

20   See: Martin J. Gössl, *Schöne, queer Zeiten?*, 22.

9. Queer Altercations

There are several queer themes that are resistant to classical attempts at scholarly classification, ignorant of the suffering they're frequently inflicting on the inquiring scholar. These are phenomena familiar to everyone in this field, but which remain unspecific, both in their origins and in their impact. Into this grouping can fall modes of behavior, norms and rules can all fall into this grouping, when they cause irritation, and when the riddles behind them can't be "solved" in any way meaningful either to heteronormative social majorities, or to the queer community. These realities are exacerbations of discourses and/or performances, generated by individuals or groups, which come about either purposefully to irritate, or as a social byproduct. These moments appear to enjoy the tensions they're grounded in, which result from the contradictions inside a queer framework, and which must be fought over—and, if necessary, tolerated—in an act of communal willpower. It's essential to recognize these conflicts—in theory and in social practice—and the opaque circumstances that they may precipitate, which can, in turn, trigger a further series of related developments:

> Gays are smarter than anyone else … . They're overrepresented as artists and inventors, and there's a reason for that. On average they have higher IQs, but also we have license to experiment and push boundaries where others don't. ... On the one hand, you have the trans lobby that's all about control and oppression and misery and victimhood and grievance culture. And then drag queens, which is about taking the same kind of pain and expressing it through gender-defying comedy and transgression and subversion. I'm very much in

the second camp. ... I see things happening first, because I'm on the edge of culture, ... I'm the canary in the coal mine.¹

The queer artist Milos Yiannopoulos knows how to provoke people, above all people from his own community. The interview with Yiannopoulos presented here prompted the editor of the queer magazine *Out* to publish an editorial note at the head of the interview—this disclaimer wanted to make absolutely clear that the views expressed by Yiannopoulos were *not* the magazine's official standpoint.²

Emanations originating in queer recognition crystallize in battle lines, which seem to want to swap moderate compromises for extreme and polarizing positions. Alternatively, such emanations harden along deep-reaching conflict lines pertaining to a heteronormative ordering system, whereby alternative solutions, offered up by subcultures, must often cede ground to the outward extensions of societal norms. All these exacerbations are strategic, shape the queer community in their discursiveness, and influence the general public. They polarize and demand confrontations with old structures, all too comfortable traditions, and unreflective patterns. Eve Kosofsky Sedgwick, a queer theoretician who's held up as the "founder of queer theory," described the concept of queerness in 1993 thus:

---

1   Chadwick Moore, "Send In the Clown: Internet Supervillain Milo Doesn't Care That You Hate Him" in: *Out Magazine* on September 21, 2016, https://www.out.com/out-exclusives/2016/9/21/send-clown-internet-supervillain-milo-doesnt-care-you-hate-him.

2   "Editor's Note: It should not need saying that the views expressed by the subject of this piece in no way represent the opinions of this magazine, but in this era of social media tribalism, the mere act of covering a contentious person can be misinterpreted as an endorsement. If LGBTQ media takes its responsibilities seriously we can't shy away from covering queer people who are at the center of this highly polarized election year, and we ask you to assess Milos Yiannopoulos, the focus of this profile, on his own words without mistaking them for ours." Chadwick Moore, Send In the Clown: Internet Supervillain Milo Doesn't Care That You Hate Him" in: *Out Magazine* on September 21, 2016, https://www.out.com/out-exclusives/2016/9/21/send-clown-internet-supervillain-milo-doesnt-care-you-hate-him.

A word so fraught as "queer" is – fraught with so many social and personal histories of exclusion, violence, defiance, excitement – never can only denote; nor even can it only connote; a part of its experimental force as a speech act is the way in which it dramatizes locutionary position itself. Anyone's use of "queer" about themselves means differently from their use of it about someone else. This is true (as it might also be true of "lesbian" or "gay") because of the violently different connotative evaluations that seem to cluster around the category. But "gay" and "lesbian" still present themselves (however delusively) as objective, empirical categories governed by empirical rules of evidence (however contested). "Queer" seems to hinge much more radically and explicitly on a person's undertaking particular, performative acts of experimental self-perception and filiation.[3]

Radicalism is inherent to what is queer, a radicalism that always knows how—at least in part—to escape the clutches of scholarly, descriptive categorizations, and creative processings. Many see the acronym LGBTI as providing a necessary counter-construct to a definition—even though others experience this same, acronymic definition as polarizing in itself. If only through the gradual extensions of the LGBTI term, it documents the social, and sometimes political needs that are met by naming processes. Many people appear to think that with the definitions L for lesbian, G for G/ay, B for bisexual, T for transgender, and I for intersexual, clear attributions have been made, which, depending on awareness levels, aim to fix, in a statistical or in a flexible manner, sexual desire or a gender-based ambiguity. Whether one agrees with this definition process or not, the discursive clarity in the terminology appellation is not contested, either in acknowledging one's own identity and desires, or in the allocation via external instances. The radicalism of the LGBTI concept lies in the social essences that are subsumed within this acronym. The letters are in no way secretive reductions, but rather, when deciphered knowledgeably, descriptions, which are backed up by a standardized narrative matrix: gay as sexual act between two men, lesbian as sexual intimacy between two women. This formula reduces things down

---

3   Eve Kosofsky Sedgwick, Tendencies (London: Routledge, 1994), 8.

to essentials, indeed, to what is perceptible, and leaves little room for maneuver for ominous interpretations. The collective clarity in decoding the LGBTI formula also becomes evident when components of the acronym are used as insults. It's only because there's an initial consensus exists, that the power of the term can establish prominence as an insult, and becomes viable in a social context:

> While there are legally registered partnerships on the one hand, and conversations are proceeding about access to marriage for lesbians and gays, and about rainbow families and rights to adopt, and while ever more Austrians speak out, in opinion polls, for further equal opportunity measures, substantial homophobic prejudices are still hovering underneath the politically correct surface.
> This cannot be a surprise to anybody: centuries of cultivated resentments do not disappear within just a few years. It is problematic, however, that in Austria hardly anyone's speaking about this dark side, about that which continues to exist, despite legal equality of opportunity. People prefer to avoid confronting homophobia, just as many people continue to avoid intervening in the case of unqualified attacks against foreigners.[4]

This phenomenon can be observed in many other postmodern, virtually interconnected societies, and not merely in Austria. This allows us to draw again on Eve Kosofsky Sedgwick's argument again: queerness's radicalism lies in its refusal to conform, which is why space must be given to exacerbations and altercations in the gay community's own discourses on the subject. And these discourses are far-reaching and polarizing, they endure for ages and are, nonetheless, continually laden with fresh emotions. They are, incontestably, present and necessary, even if they refuse categorizations—as the following, highly contentious examples are intended to demonstrate. More significant still is the function of such discourses in providing a territory that is

---

4   Irene Brickner, "Warum 'schwul' ein Schimpfwort ist" (11.01.2014), in: *Der Standard* on January 11, 2014, https://www.derstandard.at/story/1388650739347/warum-schwul-ein-schimpfwort-ist.

dangerous, in terms of the arguments that happen on it. But the danger of interpretations, falsely relayed by third parties, cannot obstruct a discourse and the arguments laid out in it—and nor can these real dangers inhibit recognition of such necessary discourses.

Trans-Formations

As a concept, transformation is founded on a plan, or at least an idea, which change ought to be achieved through which parameters. As such, transformation is determined by a point of departure and a point of arrival. One of the great, contentious debates of our times rages around gender and/or sex, transition and passing as a process with the goal of arriving, in terms of gender. From this perspective, the trans identity moment is interpreted as the metamorphosis between one gender and the other. In this, biological worlds are highly relevant, and function as maps of gender and sex, on which participants set sail and leave the one world, and are meant to steer themselves toward the other. But what in all this should be allowed to count as queer, and what matches better to a heteronormative establishment?

> At a time when many queers have signaled their desire for mainstream acceptability, it has been trans people who have carried forth the mantle of radical queerness, both personally and politically. We queer those formerly "straight" people who desire us, something I am proud to say I've done to varying degrees with every straight, cis man I've dated. We queer them when we transition, too, as when a friend dating a trans man at the start of his transition recently looked at me with a quizzical expression and said "I guess I'm queer now." It was the moment he realized that soon others would assume he had a queer history he hasn't actually lived, or began living at the moment his partner came out.[5]

---

5   Meredith Talusan, "Queer Culture in the Age of Transgender Disruption," in: *Vice*, December 12, 2016. Accessed on November 27, 2023: https://www.vice.com/en/article/aevjze/queer-culture-in-theage-of-transgender-disruptio.

Does this make a transgender biography unquestionably and permanently queer? The argument here is that the trans identity biography can be lived as a queer position, but it's also possible actors choose not to make that choice—so that in this way it's similar to a same-gender sexual orientation. Having gone through the process of gender transition does not release anybody, automatically, from a queer understanding, but a queer sense of belonging certainly is something an individual can decide to take on—or reject.

This particularly contentious part of the debate impacts above all on the question of *how long* people belong for, so it's like a debate about membership. Is queer belonging permanent and unlimited? Or should there be options of being queer once, or at times, and not at another point or other points in time? Does queerness always depend on self-definitions, or heteronomous attributions, or does it require both?

Living in solidarity in the queer milieu positively valuing—as elucidated in the above based on various arguments—subcultural and peripheral groups in all their diversity, including the alternative needs and performances pertaining to these groups. Exaggerating queer ideals based on majority-backed mechanisms of recognition might seem an attractive and comfortable strategy. But such an amplification should be understood as only one of the concepts currently available for gender-based and sexual variety. In such heteronomous determinative processes, it remains accentuated explanatory concepts, which don't have to fulfill any kind of holistic mission, but which correlate to the desire for a normative order. There's nothing reprehensible about taking on a particular concept, but excluding alternatives should be reprimanded. As such, queer belonging does not have to reflect itself in its form of appearance, but rather in everyday understandings relating to relationship forms, interpretations of gender, and sexual freedoms. This means that no one needs any kind of autonomous or heteronomous attribute, similar to a seal of approval, that confirms they're sufficiently queer. A competition to see who's the queerest of them all is also equally unnecessary, or a hierarchization regarding what is allowed to count as queer, and what's already too conformist. Because in a queer subculture, and in external perceptions of the same, all these processes lead to accentuated confrontations, which can only shrink the space needed for diverse forms of structuring—a space that's too small to begin with. This strenuous act of conscious openness becomes all the queerer, but also more polarized, the more controversial the themes addressed become: what, we ask, will trans-formation really mean for social-cultural and for political fields, including homelessness, top-flight sport, and leadership?

A Question of Age

> Queer Theory has failed to fully take account of, and incorporate, the interlocking and overlapping underpinnings of the normative frameworks by which female sexual and gender identities are constituted. There is, therefore, no "queerness" about the debate surrounding the lowering of the age of consent, and the effects on teenage boys have been over emphasized at the expense of the impact on teenage girls. In order to have a truly genuine queer debate about the age of consent, sufficient attention must be paid to all of those affected and involved, particularly girls and that the attention should be extended to schools, medical staff, social workers etc. Lowering the age of consent is likely to lead to an even greater pressure on girls to be sexually active before they are ready, exposing them to experiences and consequences before they are sufficiently emotionally and physically mature.[6]

Well into the twenty-first century's third decade, many subjects relating to sexuality remain highly emotionalized, and tabooed. Decision-makers, whether elected politicians or otherwise, like thus to delegate discourses about the same to professions and research areas that they envisage as apparently suited to handle the same, including psychiatry, law and the judiciary, and, more specifically, criminology. If any public conversations about the same take place at all, they're often conducted

---

6   Sarah Beresford, "The Age of Consent and the Ending of Queer Theory," *Laws* 3, no. 4 (2014): 773, https://doi.org/10.3390/laws3040759.

purely on a tedious, fact-based level. But this factual grind disguises that significant social and political aspects are at play:

> If the adolescent is our figure for the child, a figure intrinsically marked by a combination of protection and propulsion, qualified autonomy and peremption, we might more richly attend to axes of social difference and inequality … . This rendition of the child by- passes the somewhat overstated conclusions that white kids have futures where kids of color do not, or that innocence is only the preserve of white childhood. The conflicted, relatively recent fabrication of adolescence – as liminal, social but also biological, imitative but also inventive, vulnerable but agentive – itself invites reading difference (race, gender, class, ability, sexuality) back into rather than washed out of the theoretical framework. More avowedly than the child, the adolescent is a pluralized, resolutely historicized, and eroticized construct. While the adolescent is no less ideologically saturated than the child, the former's avowed differences – within the very category itself – engender an engagement with social inequalities more promising than add x and stir.[7]

In the book this passage is taken from, sexual theoretician Joseph Fischel argues that key categories in the debate, including childhood and youth, are loaded to the point of over spilling with norms, valuations, limitations, and much more. If these constructs seem to be clear and unitary, approaching them in the context of social reality exposes blatant differences. And it's precisely because of this fact that a queer and diverse debate is necessary. Neither demonizing nor playing down the issues involved will provide a responsible space for the discussion about sexuality and age, particularly with a view to the global gray zones, which provide possibilities for abuse, rape, coercion, and exploitation:

> It's evident that services provided by the tourism industry are also used by travelers interested in accessing child prostitutes. So there's

---

7   Joseph J. Fischel, *Sex and Harm in the Age of Consent* (Minneapolis: University of Minnesota Press, 2016), 219.

now a demand on the tourism sector, also based on international agreements, to cooperate, and to prevent the possible use of its amenities for child prostitution.[8]

Not only the tourist industry, but also many other areas of organizational and intellectual activity are now under pressure to bring in lasting improvements to the current situation. There has been an accentuated focus on perpetrators in this context—and I focus consciously on male perpetrators here, as it's primarily men who carry out the deeds in question. But focusing exclusively on these men as sick individuals falls short and is not productive in terms of illuminating the subject in the queer breadth that it requires: international politics, social work, psychotherapy, police and many further professions need a queer-theoretical consciousness regarding sexualities and genders. Only then can they draw the necessary lines between the inacceptable and the acceptable in such a way that these deeds can be prevented fundamentally—and not just deferred to different geographical localities. The queer confrontation with such sexual felonies, and with the terrible impacts that these have, must be carried out in multidimensional ways. It's necessary, for example, to recognize the fact of such modes of behavior as a reality, and not to keep silent about them out of a sense of shame, ignorance, or disinterest, and not merely to hint at them. What is required, therefore, that this subject is indeed a subject, and a clarity that abuse can never be reduced to individual perpetrators, but rather must always be viewed as part of larger systems. However unpleasant the question of age relating to sexual acts and gender-based notions may appear to some affected parties and participants, an inability to confront the issue will itself lead to more victims. This is why a mindfulness and consciousness about sexual and gender-based gray zones in the global community is necessary: in order to conduct a discourse about the same, which provides space

---

8   Astrid Winkler, "Maßnahmen gegen Kindersextourismus," in: *SWS-Rundschau (Die Zeitschrift des Vereins für interdisziplinäre sozialwissenschaftliche Studien und Analysen)* 46, no. 3 (2006), https://nbn-resolving.org/urn:nbn:de:0168-ssoar-16 4472, 313.

for prevention, intervention, and societal critique. It's crucial we create such spaces, whether people find the debate pleasant or not.

Bottom Shaming

> Bottom-shaming is nothing new and has always been partly about power. ... Some of the stigma associated with bottom-shaming is indicative of gender roles. How many times have you heard a straight person ask, "Which of you is the girl in the relationship?" The guy on the bottom is the one being penetrated, which they associate with femininity. In this society, which is more of a handicap – being a woman or being a man who exhibits a trait associated with being a woman?[9]

The division of rolls in sexual interactions between two men has been locus and content of powerful interpretations and confrontations. The defrauding of hegemonic masculinity—or so one interpretation has it—is enacted by that man who doesn't make exclusive use of his penis in satisfying his desire.[10] The division between top and bottom, active and passive, pushes inter-male sexuality in the exclusive direction of dichotomous positions, in which there's only one giver, and one receiver. This way of perceiving wants to reduce being gay, to accentuate matters so that the term only applies to a single sexual position:

> Even most rappers just used it as a neutral insult at the start, without thinking about gays. But the more massively it's used in the scene, the more it's meaning is shifted. In doing so, protagonists have assumed the aggressive, American form of homophobia. This then mixed, in some districts of Berlin, with the hatred against gays emanating from the Arabic-Turkish milieu. So that one now has to admit: the term

---

9   Jorge Rodriguez-Jimenez, "Op-ed: It Is Time to End Bottom-Shaming," in: The Out Magazine on October 31, 2014, https://www.advocate.com/31-days-prep/2014/10/31/op-ed-it-time-end-bottom-shaming.
10 See: R. W. Connell, *Masculinities*, (Hoboken: Blackwell, 2006).

definitely has a sexual referent. But the people [that use it] often don't know anybody that's openly gay. It's a bit similar to xenophobia—it's worst in areas where there are no foreigners. And as it happens, a weird rule applies [when using this term as an insult]: "you're only gay if you get fucked."[11]

It's fascinating how similar the approaches of some heteronormative and queer representatives are, in unanimously attributing true masculinity only to the active man, the one on top, or in their interpretation of the active sexual act as male performance. Indeed, it certainly is the case that understandings of roles, which stem from a heterosexual constellation of bodies—and here, too, the possible spectrum should be seen much more widely than it typically is—are applied, from without, to queer relationships, and also then internalized. A reportage on the subject for *GQ Magazine* brought a number of relevant highlights in the debate to the fore:

> David, a 35-year-old gay man from London who doesn't identify as top or bottom, says he worries that "some guys can start to define their lives" by their sexual role. "I fully understand the need to give yourself an identity, and when the only thing we all have in common (as gay men) is sex, it's the easiest one to lean on", he says. "But I also think it leans too heavily into heteronormativity, because I think it can be seen in terms of the bottom being 'the woman' and the top being 'the man'. Is there no rule book for relationships that hasn't been written by straight people?" In recent years, in some gay circles, 'bottom' has become a sneering synonym for 'camp' or 'femme-presenting'. Court, a 37-year-old gay guy from Denver, tells me that 'bottom-shaming' is definitely a thing. People feel like bottoming makes you the submissive or 'the woman, which is ridiculous', he says. But some gay guys out

---

11   Johannes Gernert, "Interview mit Marcus Staiger 'Nur wer gefickt wird, ist schwul,'" in: *Stern*, August 29, 2008. Accessed on November 27, 2023: https://www.stern.de/kultur/musik/interview-mit-marcus-staiger--nur-wer-gefickt-wird--ist-schwul--3757762.html.

there feel so threatened in their masculinity that they don't want anyone to perceive them as even being capable of taking it.[12]

This is a further case in which labeling and stigmatization is a social process, which strongly curtails the multifarious sketches that exist for representing sexuality inside a queer community. Even if self-defining one's role as either top or bottoms seems omnipresent, there's no obligation forcing you to choose between one club or the other. And there's just as little reason to give in to the pressure to sort everyone else you know or have heard of into one of the two positions. Here too, a dilemma unfolds: on the one hand, queer sexuality's true freedom is forced, by social deformations, into a heteronormative corset. On the other hand, bottom shaming's structural entrenchment in gender-based duality is testament to the fact that people only feel the need to problematize particular positions:

> Altogether, traditional masculine ideals may to some degree amplify the adverse effect that some gay men experience when compared to heterosexual men. In other words, gay men may feel pressured to live by the same expectations and restrictions that heterosexual men – whether it be as a defensive reaction or because it genuinely reflects their personality – while simultaneously experiencing some of the adverse effects of misogyny and sexual objectification that heterosexual women feel. ... Consequently, gay men who value traditional masculinity ideology may experience stress, shame, or guilt because being truly ›masculine‹ is unattainable due to their same-sex romantic attractions.[13]

---

12 Nick Levine, "It's Time to Stop Pigeonholing Gay Men as Tops and Bottoms," (23.05.2019), in: *GQ Magazine*, May 23, 2019. https://www.gq.com/story/its-time-to-stop-pigeonholing-ourselves-as-tops-and-bottoms.

13 Francisco J. Sánchez, Stefanie T. Greenberg, William Ming Liu, and Eric Vilain, "Reported Effects of Masculine Ideals on Gay Men," in *Psychology of Men & Masculinity* 10, no. 1 (2010), 10, https://doi.apa.org/doiLanding?doi=10.1037%2Fa0013513.

Concepts of a *right* kind of masculinity, as a parameter of socialization unquestionably influence the later experience of one's own gender/sex, and one's sexual preferences. To draw from the language the feminist movement, we can consider the sexual act as a mirror of our society, both in the interactions completed and the narratives that are then attached to the same. Or to articulate it more provocatively: bottom shaming is the logical consequence of heteronormative, everyday culture—and the real evidence behind the demand that the queer and the feminist movements should be drawn more tightly together in the future.

Sexual Perfectionism

If you don't have sex, you don't have a life. Whoever practices ordinary sex isn't creative. And whoever politicizes sex has no sense of fun. Popular accentuations of debates about sex in the twenty-first century uses this language, or similar, when the issue is experiencing the *right kind of* sexuality. But:

> It is not obvious whether better relations imply more sex, or more sex help build better relations. It seems likely, however, that having a positive attitude to sex, improves both how one relates to loved ones, and the amount of pleasure obtained from intimate behavior. The previous discussion suggests that sexual behavior is not functioning optimally in industrialized societies. The two most troublesome aspects are probably: (1) an elevated level of negative emotions such as guilt and shame, and (2) a malfunctioning sex life that restricts the harvesting of positive feelings. ... Whether or not present sexual behavior qualifies as a ›disease of modernity‹, there seems to be room for improvements, particularly in the form of altering the bioecological systems that drive infant development.[14]

---

14 Bjorn Grinde, "The Contribution of Sex to Quality of Life in Modern Societies," in: *Applied Research in Quality of Life* 17, 449–465 (2022). https://link.springer.com/article/10.1007%2Fs11482-021-09926-6.

Sexuality's importance for a relationship has become a commonplace. But when it comes to the question of how sexuality should be experienced, new ideals appear to stretch back, and hook up with old traditions. As is the case in the sex toy industry, which is increasingly visible, and which, with its desire-inducing innovations knows how to entertain virtually interconnected, postmodern societies:

> Many varying sex toy industries appear to be rising. With many individuals stay at home either with someone else or by themselves, sales of sex toys have increased. Items and media designed arouse sexually have often circulated in society. ... Besides, technology trends and various consumers prevalent in the area are also enhancing the market framework. Moreover, countries like Germany, Denmark, and Holland are certainly the main growing states pushing the demand for sexual toy products in Europe. ... Another different factor being followed by the vendors is the enduring uncovered opportunity of more comprehensively serving women through gender-neutral tones, which likely contributes to the growth of the market. ... The high demand for sex toys by NGOs, government, and foundations for supplying amidst many countries is a significant factor that will contribute to the increasing requirement for condoms. As final consumers are now becoming clear to experiment and adventurous, the need for future fashion and provoking sensual undies is multiplying in the market report. The need for sexual emollients has mainly been concentrated in European countries. The need for other goods which majorly includes sexual improvement supplements is also growing at a stable pace. The European sexual health market is witnessing a high need for herbal goods as they are without side effects, which is contrary to allopathic products. ... In Europe, the sexual wellbeing market is experiencing a shift because of the further introduction of female sexual products for example, vibrators, female condoms, and dildos. ... New innovations and technology arrivals in manufacturing

sex toys like 3D printing and production of organic emollients are running the business in Germany ... .[15]

This is not simply commercial interests discovering new forms of desire, including the female body, previously *terra incognita*, alongside the commercial idealization of male penetration. Moreover, new ways of producing a desirous finale have moved to the center of companies' economic interests. This has made the products not only more various, but also technologically more complex, of higher quality, and more attractive in the forms they assume. Utensils for male sexuality have risen up above the smelly 1970s nylon air, and are now color-coordinated, packed in enticing forms, advertised in entertaining video clips, and discreetly sold. Their message is thereby clear: sex takes place between maximum two people, is good, clean fun, and is part and parcel of modern life—or at least of *normal* modern life. And sex may now be undertaken alone—so this message continues—and particularly for these purposes there are a number of expensive supporting aids you can buy, which all promise you an absolute profit in terms of desire. Whether alone or in company, sexuality is regarded as a healthy activity within modern existence, which intrinsically contains a feeling of wellbeing within it. Or, as Alexandra Fine, a sex toy producer puts it, a "mix of at-home entertainment and at-home wellness."[16] And the description really does fit to a tee, in order to successfully sell one's products to the women and me, both queer and nonqueer, who are being targeted. Sports socks for youngsters have had their time, and the cucumber stays in the fridge: quite consciously, people are saying goodbye to old images (and some genuinely useful tools among them), in order to buy stimulating high-tech and sexy design instead. Customers are sold the promise and the ideology that good sex

---

15 Yeshwant Naik, "Regulations on Sex Toy Industry in Europe," in: *Technium Social Sciences Journal*, 16 (2021), 171n., https://techniumscience.com/index.php/social sciences/issue/view/32.
16 Rosemary Donahue, "Even the Worst Year Ever Was No Match for the Sexual Wellness Industry," in: *allure* on January 24, 2021. https://www.allure.com/gall ery/sexu al-wellness-sex-toy-sales-skyrocketed-during-pandemic.

lies in one's own hands, and ought to be permanently reinvented, in order not to count as prudish, and also not to miss out on your ultimate reward for all that work. On this view, sex is above all your path to climaxing.

For long, ideas and feelings about sexual perfectionism were co-shaped by actual possibilities of sexual performance, i.e. from actual, anatomical possibilities of uniting together with another person, either anally or vaginally. This subject continues to dominate, which explains the current but simultaneously archaic cult that surrounds the erection. Bodies, however, and the sexuality connected to them, have changed, both in economic terms and in social perceptions. Well-being, health, relaxation, creativity, and self-determination are only some of the rallying cries that are linked intentionally with the purchasing of sex toys. Without such supports, sex is portrayed as reduced to a dull, obligatory act: lethargic rather than agile, gray instead of colorful, strenuous, but not energetic:

> Our contemporary daily lives are flooded with sexual stimuli, but also emptied of the same. ... Clearly eroticism and desire are driven away much more effectively by their own hyperbolic, cultural staging, their almost ceaseless commercialization and electronic dissemination, than they ever where by old forms of repression through bans. ... Everything has become commonplace, everything seems to be slotted in and frozen, but then something unpredictable, shocking, and mad happens. Suddenly, fantasies of omnipotence and perfection are back. Things no longer proceed smugly, but rather in a highly risky way; boredom no longer prevails, but rather a state of emergency.[17]

This analysis does indeed seem relevant, to name and describe the accentuation toward sexual perfection, and the hidden paradox within that. Many seem to feel they can't live up to such perfectionistic ideas about sex, or don't want to become slaves to sexual pressure. The feeling, that

---

17   Volkmar Sigusch, "Kultureller Wandel der Sexualität," in *Sexuelle Störungen und ihre Behandlungen*, ed. Volkmar Sigusch, (Stuttgart: Vandenhoeck & Ruprecht, 2007), 24.

one's own sex life is lacking something grows alongside the demands involved in paying for dispensers of desire—sex toys and the like—to plug this gap. To the image of idealized vitality has now been added the facet of *healthy* sexuality, which, implicitly and sometimes explicitly, washes around everyday life. In response, the accentuated development in relation to queer recognition can mean that not experiencing sexuality at all, or even a justified rejection of sex toys and sex entertainment, is actually queerer than it looks—considering the unknowns pertaining to production, unresolved issues of resource sustainability, and questionable labor conditions.

10. Queer Envy of Recognition

Questions as to why Queer Studies, or indeed other research on gender, sex and sexuality is needed in the first place, expose perfidious strategies, embedded in past, present, and future power structures, of tabooing elementary areas of life, thus blocking necessary processes of recognition. Opponents and critics abruptly demand an obligation to present arguments for, and thus justify this area of studies—while papering over the fact that no such necessity for this justification exists. These forms of hierarchization and recognition have been researched only too well. They're well-known strategies, and part of powerful, societal confrontations.

The sociocultural areas of life presented here are not only real and essential, but also provide, in their very existence, arguments enough for a scholarly investigation of the subject matter. In a manifold world, with a high number of explanatory approaches to match, there simply are many possible points of departure on the journey of representing connections. The queer departure point is neither more illuminating nor, in itself, more profound than other perspectives. But it is nearer the lifeworlds of some subcultures and thus possibly more relevant. Pressure is put on this argumentative clarity, which has combined with a rejection of social-historical colonialism, by culturally dominant standard values. This is why taking on and keeping hold of a queer standpoint means a form of exertion relevant to our subjects: personal, cultural, social, political, and academic.

Recognizing a subject does not automatically and immediately mean a demand that values acceptance of the same. Rather, the first step is to develop a differentiated perception of the subject itself. Wealth, success, entertainment, sexuality, beauty, and culture, and the peculiar exaggerations and confrontations pertaining to the same, are all queer appearance forms, represented in a subcultural community, and reflected by—and reflected on—by many individuals. Queer recognition means providing reflective space for facts, contextualizations, and a flowing discourse. The visibility of these elements encompasses both majority-based and subcultural dimensions, and real and virtual ones. It is co-shaped by every utterly personal action, and not just from superordinated collectives. Positive appreciations, but also disdain and slights, permanently contribute countless facets to queer dynamics of recognition, and decide at an individual level, and in observing a group, which recognition mechanisms assume clear outlines, and which evaporate or become marginalized. Actors attribute slights and contempt all too easily to societal majorities. But, as demonstrated in the deliberations presented here, this doesn't quite fit the bill. Instead, passing the buck for one's own mistakes, and a general lack of solidarity, onto others, is an established appeasement strategy used by queer community representatives. There are those who move within queer communities in a conformist ways, and there's also the option of experiencing some of queerness's social and cultural facets, while ignoring other areas that seem inappropriate or unpleasant. This strategy allows actors to see their own *otherness* as the right kind, and gives people the strength of showing solidarity for one cross-section of the queer community that fits them—and for individuals to master the task of establishing themselves within nonqueer everyday society.

However, it's precisely out of such a strategy that two well-known danger zones can develop: oppressive heteronormativity, and overwhelming queerness. Participants are threatened with existing precariously between both worlds. Nonqueer, achievement-based society on the one hand, in which one can take part, on an equal footing, without an admission of queerness. And queer subculture on the other, which provides opportunities for sexual, emotional and cultural desire, but which can overstretch possibly existing areas of tolerance for accepted queerness. Thus, it's not merely so-called Minority Stress, the stress of being constantly decoded and judged as a minority,[1] which unleashes repercussions to match, but also internalized norms held by social majorities, which are accompanied by a major lack of understanding for the unconventional totality of queer subculture. In consequence, the thought of belonging to a minority is only oppressive because the minority expands—in manifold, expressive ways, and so uncontrolled by its own ideals, and normative idealizations.

Various psychological tests have attempted to do justice to these perceptive worlds, and their internal and external changes:

> More recently, scales have been designed to include assessment of attitudes toward and among bisexuals as well as gay men and lesbians ... or to address this group specifically ... . The stigma associated with bisexuality, though similar to homosexual stigma, has an added component of perceived instability or lack of legitimacy ... . Indeed, bisexuals are often targets of prejudice from heterosexuals as well as gay men and lesbians who perceive bisexuality as a transitional or opportunistic identity ... . Discrepancies between low levels of self-reported homophobia and observed behaviors have been documented and are arguably due to the fact that existing scales assess specific types of homonegativity that are no longer endorsed among the undergraduate samples typically studied ... . Indeed, cultural acceptance has quickly outdated older scales, such that many items ... appear extreme and are unlikely to be endorsed, particularly among university students. Rather than disappearing, LGB-bias has transformed over time. Hence, newer scales have been designed to assess these more subtle, modern attitudes toward LGB individuals ... .[2]

---

1 See: Ilan H. Meyer, "Minority Stress and Mental Health in Gay Men," in: *Journal of Health and Social Behavior* 36, no. 1 (1995), 38ff., https://doi.org/10.2307/2137286.

2 William S. Ryan and Jim Blascovich, "Measures of Attitudes towards Sexual Orientation: Heterosexism, Homophobia, and Internalized Stigma, in: *Measures of Personality and Social Psychological Constructs*, ed. Gregory J. Boyle et al., (London: Elsevier Academic Press, 2015), 721.

Minority stress can easily be understood as a logical outcome, when the absence of equal recognition for alternative forms for relationships, and for lives, are considered. But the lack of understanding for the non-conforming totality of queer subculture is harder to grasp. This is why, in the following, I name this phenomena the queer envy of recognition, and attempt to explain the same.

The model of a queer, recognition-based envy is the theoretical attempt to explain why certain queer individuals refuse an apparently logical queer solidarity. In so doing, the crossing of boundaries pertaining to heteronormative appreciation constitutes decisive corridors of demarcation for emotional transfer: regarding disdain, rejection, and aggression. These corridors are only positions in an ostensible sense: the queer game surrounding heteronormative recognition is much more like an individually constructed island, surrounded by fluid possibilities. On this island, participants search for political, social and cultural commonalities, but also mark down where distinctions should be made, but without even being able to name an opponent in the discourse. The only thing that's accepted as a solid foundation is desire, and it's out of this desire that the individual island expands into a collective terrain. This location is not merely a delimited and constrained space, but also a terrain of silent desire. The stability of the island soil may communicate a feeling of purchase and of clarity, and may therefore feel more pleasant than the endless depth and vastness of the waters surrounding, but the feeling of comfort is deceptive: the shifting sands of a heteronormative continental shelf provide neither constant certainty nor sufficient space for the multifariousness in the ocean depths. People on the island are permanently in danger of either sinking into the sands, or of being swallowed up by the rising tides.

The desire to be completely *normal* remains unfulfillable in queer existence, and yet it's a concept that some want to chase after forever—or feel they have to. But concurrently, the desire exists for that other life, for queer freedom, for life without bourgeois obligation. Actors look up with envy to those who manage to keep their distance from this normative terrain, thus enjoying gender-based and sexual fluidity to the full. But the coercions, expectations and structures of the heteronormative everyday can be felt all too often: the unknown depths that are encountered reflect both anxiety and attraction. It's only the thought of betraying opportunities for subcultural participation to normative majority-backed structures that prevents participants from giving in to this envious desire.

Queer, recognition-based envy reveals people's greed for superordinated appreciation, meaning that all esteem attached to queer disorder is eyed up enviously. Recognizing queer others means reducing one's own capacity to conform to the norm, and reduces the appreciation shown for the subjugation presented. This humiliation leads to distancing, disdain, and animosity within the queer community—if only through this, it knows it will be appreciated by its own heteronormative equivalent. Queer, recognition-based envy is a pendulum swinging between one's own wish to unfold freely as an individual, and the overwhelming greed/need to be valued for conforming. The reference object thereby is as both arbitrarily selected and exchangeable, part of a fluid queerness surrounding the island of the heteronormative personality: well-being, wealth, success, entertainment, sexuality, beauty, culture, and communal accentuations bear witness to the (un)-articulated discourses that envelop queer, recognition-based envy.

Bibliography

Altman, Dennis. "What Changed in the Seventies." in: *Homosexuality: Power and Politics*, edited by Gay Left Collective, 52–63. London, New York: Allison & Busby, 1980.

Badgett, M.V. Lee, Holning Lau, Brad Sears, and Deborah Ho. *Bias in the Workplace: Consistent Evidence of Sexual Orientation and Gender Identity Discrimination*. Los Angeles: UCLA, The Williams Institute, 2007. https://escholarship.org/uc/item/5h3731xr.

Bailey, Robert W. "Sexual Identity and Urban Space, Economic Structure and Political Action." in: *Sexual Identities, Queer Politics*, edited by Mark Blasius, 231–255. New Jersey: Princeton University Press, 2001.

Battles, Kathleen and Wendy Hilton-Morrow. "Gay Characters in Conventional Spaces: Will and Grace and the Situation Comedy Genre." *Critical Studies in Media Communication* 19, no. 1 (2002): 101n. https://doi.org/10.108 0/07393180216553.

Beresford, Sarah. "The Age of Consent and the Ending of Queer Theory." *Laws* 3, no. 4 (2014): 760–779. https://doi.org/10.3390/laws3040759.

Bernhard, Christoph Bernhard. "Wohlstand wichtiger als Einkommen für Zufriedenheit mit der finanziellen Situation: Untersuchungen zur Zufriedenheit mit der finanziellen Situation im europäischen Vergleich." *Informationsdienst Soziale Indikatoren (ISI)*, no. 26 (2001): 12–15. https://doi.org/10.15464/isi.26.2001.12-15.

Binson, Diane, William J. Woods, Lance Pollack, Jay Paul, Ron Stall, and Joseph A. Catania. "Differential HIV Risk in Bathhouses and Public Cruising Areas," *American Journal of Public Health* 91, no. 9

(2001): 1482–1486. https://ajph.a phapublications.org/doi/10.2105/ AJPH.91.9.1482.

Böcker, Anna. *Weder gleich- noch que(e)rstellen. Heteronormativität, Reproduktion und Citizenship in den Debatten zur Lebenspartnerschaft.* Berlin: Gender Politik Online, 2011. https://www.fu-berlin.de/sites/gpo/pol_sys/politikfelder/Weder_gleich_noch_queerstellen/annaboeckerglecihnochqueerstellen.pdf.

Brown, Anna. "5 key findings about LGBT Americans." *Pew Research Center*, June 13, 2017, https://www.pewresearch.org/fact-tank/2017/06/13/5-key-findingsabout-lgbt-americans/.

Butler, Judith. *Gender Trouble: Feminism and the Subversion of Identity.* New York: Routledge, 2006.

Butler, Judith. "Imitation and Gender Insubordination." in: *The Lesbian and Gay Studies Reader*, edited by Henry Abelove, Michele Barale, and David Halperin, 307–320. New York: Routledge, 1993.

Carpenter, Dale. "The Unknown Past of Lawrence v. Texas." *Michigan Law Review* 102, no. 7 (2004): 1464–1527. https://doi.org/10.2307/4141912.

Carter, David. *Stonewall, The Riots that sparked the Gay Revolution.* New York: Macmillan 2004.

Chong-suk, Han and Choi Kyung-Hee. "Very Few People Say 'No Whites': Gay Men of Color and The Racial Politics of Desire." *Sociological Spectrum* 38, no. 3 (2018): 145–161, https://doi.org/10.1080/02732173.2018.1469444.

Cole, Shaun. *"Don We Now Our Gay Apparel": Gay Men's Dress in the Twentieth Century.* Oxford: Berg, 2000.

Connell, R.W. *Masculinities.* Hoboken: Blackwell, 2006.

Crookston, Cameron, ed. *The Cultural Impact of RuPaul's Drag Race.* Chicago: Chicago University Press, 2021.

D'Emilio, John. "Capitalism and Gay Identity." in: *The Lesbian and Gay Studies Reader*, edited Henry Abelove, Michele Aina Barale, and David M. Halperin, 467–476. New York: Routledge, 1993.

Dib, Hiba and Lester W Johnson. "Gay Male Consumers Seeking Identity in Luxury Consumption: The Self-Concept." *International Journal of Business Marketing and Management (IJBMM)* 4, no. 2 (2019): 25–39.

Ecke, Matthias and Sebastian Petzold. "Die Vermessung des Fortschritts, Konkurrierende Strategien zur Verallgemeinerung widerstreiten der Wachstumsverständnisse." in: *Wohlstand, Wachstum, Investitionen, Junge Wissenschaft für wirtschaftlichen und sozialen Fortschritt, WISO Diskurs, Expertisen und Dokumentationen zur Wirtschafts- und Sozialpolitik*, edited by Abteilung Wirtschafts- und Sozialpolitik der Friedrich-Ebert-Stiftung, 9–21. Bonn: Friedrich Ebert, 2012.

Eco, Umberto. *On Beauty: A History of a Western Idea*. Translated by Alastair McEwen. London: Seeker & Warburg, 2004.

Emslie, Carol, Jemma Lennox, and Lana Ireland. "The role of alcohol in identity construction among LGBT people: a qualitative study." *Sociology of Health & Illness* 39, no. 8 (2017): 1465–1479. https://pubmed.ncbi.nlm.nih.gov/28833252/.

Fauck, Silvia. *Mid Love Crisis, Beziehungstipps für Fortgeschrittene*. Munich: Piper, 2020.

Feinberg, Leslie Feinberg. "Youth of color form STAR – Street Transvestite Action Revolutionaries, Lavender & red, part 73." *Workers World*, September 24, 2006. https://workers.org/2006/us/lavender-red-73/.

Fischel, Joseph J. *Sex and Harm in the Age of Consent*. Minneapolis: University of Minnesota Press, 2016.

Foley, B. Fergus. "Significant Others: Gay Subcultural Histories and Practices." PhD diss., Simon Fraser University, 1987.

Foucault, Michel. *The History of Sexuality, Volume I: An Introduction*. Translated by Robert Hurley. New York: Pantheon Books, 1978.

Fredriksen-Goldsen, Karen I., Hyun-Jun Kim, and Susan E. Barkan. "Disability Among Lesbian, Gay, and Bisexual Adults: Disparities in: Prevalence and Risk." *American Journal of Public Health* 102, no. 1 (2012): e16-e21. https://www.ncbi.nlm.nih.gov/pmc/articles/PMC3490559/.

Giddens, Anthony. *The Transformation of Intimacy, Sexuality, Love and Eroticism in Modern Societies*. Stanford: Stanford University Press, 1992.

Gössl, Martin J. "Dark/Backrooms: The Meaning of Queer Spaces of Sex." https://www.research gate.net/publication/328686195.

Gössl, Martin J. *Eine praxisbezogene Perspektive auf die Gender und Queer Studies*. Bielefeld: transcript, 2014.

Grinde, Bjorn. "The Contribution of Sex to Quality of Life in Modern Societies." *Applied Research in Quality of Life* 17, (2022): 449–465, https://l ink.springer.com/article/10.1007%2Fs11482-021-09926-6.

Groh-Samberg, Olaf and Florian R. Hertel. "Ende der Aufstiegsgesellschaft?" *APuZ aktuell, Aus Politik und Zeitgeschichte*, February 27, 2015, https://www.bpb.de/shop/zeitschriften/apuz/201649/ende-de r-aufstiegsgesellschaft/.

Gross, Larry. "What Is Wrong with This Picture? Lesbian Women and Gay Men on Television," in: *Queer Words, Queer Images, Communication and the Construction of Homosexuality*, edited by R. Jeffrey Ringer, 143–157. New York: NYU Press, 1994.

Guzy, Lidia. "Tabu–Die kulturelle Grenze im Körper." in: *Geschlecht als Tabu: Orte, Dynamiken und Funktionen der De/Thematisierung von Geschlecht*, edited by Ute Frietsch, Konstanze Hanitzsch, Jennifer John, and Beatrice Michaelis, 17–22. Bielefeld: transcript, 2008.

Halperin, David M. *How to be Gay*. Cambridge, Massachusetts: Belknap Press, 2012.

Henderson, Linda. *Love and Money, Queer, Class, and Cultural Production*. New York: 2013.

Honneth, Axel. *Das Recht der Freiheit, Grundriss einer demokratischen Sittlichkeit*. Frankfurt: Suhrkamp, 2011

Horn, Anita. Anerkennung und Freiheit, Subjekttheoretische Grundlagen einer Theorie demokratischer Sittlichkeit," *Archiv für Rechts- und Sozialphilosophie (ARSP)* 104, no. 1 (2018): 16–40. https://doi.org/10.51 67/uzh-123911.

Jagose, Annamarie. *Queer Theory, An Introduction*. New York: New York University Press, 1996.

Langens, Thomas A. "Leistung." In *Handbuch der Allgemeinen Psychologie – Motivation und Emotion*, edited by Veronika Brandstätter and Jürgen H. Otto, 217–224. Göttingen: Hogrefe, 2009.

MacRae, Andrea Pauline. "Hegemonic negotiation and LGBT representation in contemporary teen films." PhD diss., University of Western Australia, 2018.

Marcus, Eric. *Making Gay History, The Half-Century Fight for Lesbian and Gay Equal Rights*. New York: Harper Perennial, 2002.

Mattson, Greggor. "Are Gay Bars Closing? Using Business Listings to Infer Rates of Gay Bar Closure in the United States, 1977–2019." *Socius: Sociological Research for a Dynamic World* 5, (2019). https://doi.org/10.1177/2378023119 894832.

Meyer, Ilan H. "Minority Stress and Mental Health in Gay Men," in: *Journal of Health and Social Behavior* 36, no. 1 (1995), 38–56, https://doi.org/10.2307/2137286.

Mitchell, Christopher A. "The Transformation of Gay Life from the Closet to Liberation, 1948–1980: New York City's Gay Markets as a Study in Late Capitalism." PhD diss., State University of New Jersey, 2015.

Movement Advancement Project and Center for American Progress. *Paying an unfair Price: The Financial Penalty for LGBT Women in America*. Denver: Center for American Progress, 2015.

Naik, Yeshwant. "Regulations on Sex Toy Industry in Europe." *Technium Social Sciences Journal* 16 (2021), 168–174. https://techniumscience.com/index.php/socialsciences/issue/view/32.

Nothing, Ehn. *Street Transvestite Action Revolutionaries: Survival, Revolt, and Queer Antagonist Struggle*. New York: Untorelli Press 2013. Available as PDF: https://untorellipress.noblogs.org/files/2011/12/STAR.pdf,12.

Peele, Thomas. "Introduction: Popular Culture, Queer Culture." in: *Queer Popular Culture, Literature, Media, Film, and Television*, edited by Thomas Peele, 1–8. New York: Springer, 2007.

Plummer, Ken. "Critical Sexualities Studies." In *The Wiley-Blackwell Companion to Sociology*, edited by G. Ritzer, 243–268. Hoboken: Wiley-Blackwell, 2011. https://doi.org/10.1002/9781444347388.ch14.

Posch, Waltraud. *Projekt Körper. Wie der Kult um die Schönheit unser Leben prägt*. Frankfurt: Campus, 2009.

Raab, Heike. "Sexual Politics, juridische Emanzipationsdiskurse und Staat." PhD diss., University of Vienna, 2009.

Ream, Geoffrey L. and Nicholas Forge. "Homeless lesbian, gay, bisexual and transgender (LGBT) youth in New York City: Insights from the field." *Child Welfare* 93, no. 2 (2014): 7–22.

Reiber, Chris and Justin R. Garcia. "Hooking up: Gender differences, evolution, and pluralistic ignorance." *Evolutionary Psychology* 8, no. 3, (2010): 390–404.

Ridge, Damien, Amos Hee, and Victor Minichiello. "Asian Men on the Scene." *Journal of Homosexuality* 36, no. 3–4 (1999), 43–68. https://www.tandfonli ne.com/doi/abs/10.1300/J082v36n03_03.

Roseneil, Sasha. "Queer Individualization: The Transformation of Personal Life in the Early 21st Century." *NORA—Nordic Journal of Women's Studies* 15, no. 2–3 (2007): 84–99. https://doi.org/10.1080/08038740701482952.

Rubin, Gayles S. "Thinking Sex: Notes for a Radical Theory of the Politics of Sexuality." in: *The Lesbian and Gay Studies Reader*, edited Henry Abelove, Michele Aina Barale and David M. Halperin, 3–44. New York: Routledge, 1993.

Russell, Jamie. *Queer Burroughs*. New York: Palgrave MacMillan, 2001.

Ryan, William S. and Jim Blascovich. "Measures of Attitudes towards Sexual Orientation: Heterosexism, Homophobia, and Internalized Stigma," in: *Measures of Personality and Social Psychological Constructs*, edited by Gregory J. Boyle et al., 719–751. London: Elsevier Academic Press, 2015.

Sánchez, Francisco J., Stefanie T. Greenberg, William Ming Liu, and Eric Vilain. "Reported Effects of Masculine Ideals on Gay Men." *Psychology of Men & Masculinity* 10, no. 1 (2010): 73–87. https://doi.apa.org/doiLanding?doi=10.1037%2Fa0013513.

Sedgwick, Eve Kosofsky. *Tendencies*. London: Routledge, 1994.

Sigusch, Volkmar. "Kultureller Wandel der Sexualität." in: *Sexuelle Störungen und ihre Behandlungen*, edited by Volkmar Sigusch, 8–26. Stuttgart: Vandenhoeck & Ruprecht, 2007.

Sturgis, Matthew. *Oscar: A Life*. London: Apollo, 2018.

Tseng, Wei-Hong. "'NO ASIANS PLEASE,' 'ONLY FOR ASIANS': Experiences of East-Asian Gay Newcomers on Grindr and Jack'd in London." PhD Diss., Goldsmiths University of London, 2017.

Wade, Ryan and Gary Harper. "Racialized Sexual Discrimination (RSD) in the Age of Online Sexual Networking: Are Young Black Gay/Bisexual Men (YBGBM) at Elevated Risk for Adverse Psychological

Health?" *American Journal of Community Psychology* 65, no. 3–4 (2019): 504–523. https://doi.org/10.1002/aj cp.12401.

Wagenknecht, Peter. "Was ist Heteronormativität? Zu Geschichte und Gehalt des Begriffs." in: *Heteronormativität, Empirische Studien zu Geschlecht, Sexualität und Macht*, edited by Jutta Hartmann, Christian Klesse, Peter Wagenknecht, Bettina Fritzsche and Kristina Hackmann, 17–34. Wiesbaden: Springer, 2007.

Warner, Michael. "Introduction." in: *Fear of a Queer Planet: Queer Politics and Social Theory*, edited by Michael Warner, vii-xxxi. Minneapolis: University of Minnesota, 2004.

Warner, Michael. "Pleasures and Dangers of Shame." in: *Gay Shame*, edited by David M. Halperin and Valerie Traub, 283–296. Chicago: University of Chicago Press, 2009.

Warner, Michael. *The Trouble with Normal: Sex, Politics, and the Ethics of Queer Life*. Cambridge: Harvard University Press, 1999.

Williams Institute, The, at the UCLA School of Law. "LGBT Demographic Data Interactive." 2019. https://williamsinstitute.law.ucla.edu/visua lizati on/lgbt-stats/?topic=LGBT#about-the-data.

Winkler, Astrid. "Maßnahmen gegen Kindersextourismus." *SWS-Rundschau (Die Zeitschrift des Vereins für interdisziplinäre sozialwissenschaftliche Studien und Analysen)* 46, no. 3 (2006): 305–329. https://nbn-resolv ing.org/urn:nbn:de:0168-ssoar-164472.

News or Magazine Articles

APA, Editors at. "Ende des Life Balls: Das sind die wahren Gründe für das Aus." *Vienna Online*, May 20, 2019. https://www.vienna.at/ende-des-life-balls-das-sind-die-wahren-gruende-fuer-das-aus/6214286.

Are, Carolina. "How 'RuPaul's Drag Race' changed the way we speak." *Quartz Media Inc.*, October 2, 2019. https://qz.com/quartzy/1715788/how-rupauls-drag-race-made-lgbtq-culture-mainstream/.

Brickner, Irene. "Warum 'schwul' ein Schimpfwort ist." *Der Standard*, January 11, 2014. https://www.derstandard.at/story/1388650739347/wa rum-schwul-ein-schimpfwort-ist.

Caron, Christina. "L.G.B.T.Q. People Face Increased Risks From Covid, but Many Don't Want the Vaccine." *New York Times*, May 5, 2021. https://www.nytimes.com/2021/03/05/well/lgbtq-covid-19-vaccine.html?referringSource=articleShare.

Carter, David. "Exploding the Myths of Stonewall." *Gay City News*, June 27, 2019. https://www.gaycitynews.com/exploding-the-myths-of-stonewall/.

Chew-Bose, Durga. "The Androgynous Beauty Mood of the Moment, The blurred lines between feminine and masculine is a blasé bending of expectations." *Flare*, November 27, 2014. https://www.flare.com/beauty/the-androgynous-beauty-mood-of-the-moment/.

Colvin, Caroline. "Am I Queer? Here's How To Tell, According To Sexuality Experts." *Elite Daily*, August 19, 2019. https://www.elitedaily.com/p/am-i-queer-heres-how-to-tell-according-to-sexuality-experts-18649786.

Connor, Christopher T. "How the gay party scene short-circuited and became a moneymaking bonanza." *Conversation*, February 12, 2021. https://theconversation.com/how-the-gay-party-scene-short-circuited-and-became-a-moneymaking-bonanza-153424.

Donahue, Rosemary. "Even the Worst Year Ever Was No Match for the Sexual Wellness Industry." *Allure*, January 24, 2021. https://www.allure.com/gallery/sexual-wellness-sex-toy-sales-skyrocketed-during-pandemic.

Faiola, Anthony. "British Conservatives lead charge for gay marriage." *Washington Post*, March 29, 2012. https://www.washingtonpost.com/world/british-conservatives-lead-charge-for-gay-marriage/2012/03/29/gIQAzatzjS_story.html.

Flores, Buffy. "This 'No Fats, No Fems' Shirt Is Everything That's Wrong With the Gay Community." *Pride*, April 28, 2016. https://www.pride.com/firstperson/2016/4/28/no-fatsno-fems-shirt-everything-thats-wrong-gay-community.

Gernert, Johannes. "Interview mit Marcus Staiger, 'Nur wer gefickt wird, ist schwul.'" *Stern*, August 29, 2008. https://www.stern.de/kultur/musik/interview-mit-marcus-staiger--nur-wer-gefickt-wird--ist-schwul--3757762.html.

Gilbert, Sky. "Is queer culture losing its radical roots?" *Conversation*, June 19, 2018. https://theconversation.com/is-queer-culture-losing-its-radical-roots-97837.

James, Scott. "There Goes the Gayborhood." *New York Times*, June 21, 2021. https://www.nytimes.com/2017/06/21/us/gay-pride-lgbtq-gayborhood.html.

Lamot, Tom. "Tom Daley: 'I'm only recognised when strangers think of me in my pants.'" *Guardian*, February 22, 2020. https://www.theguardian.com/sport/2020/feb/22/tom-daley-only-recognised-strangers-think-of-me-in-my-pants.

Levine, Nick Levine. "It's Time to Stop Pigeonholing Gay Men as Tops and Bottoms." *GQ Magazine*, May 23, 2019. https://www.gq.com/story/its-time-to-stop-pigeonholing-ourselves-as-tops-and-bottoms.

Lim, Gene, Brady Robards, and Bronwyn Carlson. "Grindr is deleting its 'ethnicity filter.' But racism is still rife in online dating." *Conversation*, June 7, 2020. https://theconversation.com/grindr-is-deleting-its-ethnicityfilter-but-racism-is-still-rife-in-online-dating-140077.

McGee, Jordan. "Confident and Comfortable: The Beauty of Androgyny." *Grand Central Magazine*, February 15, 2017. http://gcmag.org/confident-and-comfortable-the-beauty-of-androgyny/.

Moore, Chadwick. "Send In the Clown: Internet Supervillain Milo Doesn't Care That You Hate Him." *Out Magazine*, September 21, 2016. https://www.out.com/out-exclusives/2016/9/21/send-clown-internet-supervillain-milo-doesnt-care-you-hate-him.

Mulkerrins, Jane. "'We had death threats': the defiant return of Will & Grace, The groundbreaking TV show returns to tackle Trump, butt doubles and Madonna-bashing millennials." *Guardian*, January 20, 2018. https://www.theguardian.com/culture/2018/jan/20/we-had-death-threats-the-defiant-return-of-will-grace.

Pyzyk, Katie. "The disappearance of the modern-day 'gayborhood.'" *Smart Cities Dive*, November 7, 2017. https://www.smartcitiesdive.com/news/the-disappearance-of-the-modern-day-gayborhood/510134/.

Reddish, David. "Are drag queens modern-day shamans? Alaska takes us to the church of drag comedy." *Queerty*, April 24, 2021. https://ww

w.queerty.com/drag-queens-modern-day-shamans-alaska-takes-us-church-drag-comedy-20210414.

Reuters. "Iceland's gay PM marries partner under new law." *Reuters*, June 28, 2010. https://www.reuters.com/article/idINIndia-49721320100628.

Rodriguez-Jimenez, Jorge. "Op-ed: It Is Time to End Bottom-Shaming." *Out Magazine*, October 31, 2014. https://www.advocate.com/31-days-prep/2014/10/31/op-ed-it-time-end-bottom-shaming.

Staples, Louis. "Did culture really embrace queer people this decade?" *BBC Culture*, December 26, 2019. https://www.bbc.com/culture/article/20191218-the-decade-that-saw-queerness-go-mainstream.

Sunderland, Ruth. "After the crash, Iceland's women lead the rescue." *Guardian*, March 21, 2009. https://www.theguardian.com/world/2009/feb/22/iceland-women.

Talusan, Meredith. "Queer Culture in the Age of Transgender Disruption." *Vice*, December 20, 2016. https://www.vice.com/en/article/aevjze/queer-culture-in-the-age-of-transgender-disruption.

Wilchins, Riki. "A Women for Her Time." *Village Voice*, February 26, 2002. https://www.villagevoice.com/2002/02/26/a-woman-for-her-time/.

Wong, Alia. "Gay Pride parades used to mean protests. Now they're an excuse for straight kids to party." *USA Today*, June 4, 2019. https://www.usatoday.com/story/news/LGBT-issues/2018/06/22/pride-parades-excuse-straight-kids-party/712068002/.

Digital: Reference Works, Platforms and Organizations

Alaska Thunderfuck, https://alaskathunderfuck.com/.
Council on Social Work Education, https://www.cswe.org/Centers-Initiatives/Initiatives/Clearinghouse-for-Economic-Well-Being/Working-Definition-of-Economic-Well-Being.
Courtney Watson, www.doorwaytherapeutics.com/about/.
Duden, https://www.duden.de/rechtschreibung/Leistung.
Ginger's, https://www.lesbianbarproject.com/gingers.

Jack'd, https://www.jackd.com/.
Kindr Gindr, https://www.kindr.grindr.com/.
Lilian Rubin, https://lillianrubin.com/.
Logo, http://www.logotv.com/.
MAP, movement advancement project, LGBT People with Disabilities, https://www.lgbtmap.org/file/LGBT-People-With-Disabilities.pdf.
Paris is burning, https://www.imdb.com/title/tt0100332/.
Randy Wicker, Vimeo.com, https://vimeo.com/37548074.
Tom Daley Channel, https://www.youtube.com/watch?v=OJwJnoB9EKw.
Will & Grace, https://www.imdb.com/title/tt0157246/.

Index

A

Abelove, Henry, 27, 34, 70
Altman, Dennis, 83
Are, Carolina, 56

B

Badgett, M.V. Lee, 24, 25
Bailey, Robert W., 72
Barale, Michele, 27, 34, 70
Barkan, Susan E., 102
Battles, Kathleen, 98
Beresford, Sarah, 119
Bernhard, Christoph, 29
Binson, Diane, 63
Blascovich, Jim, 133
Blasius, Mark, 72
Böcker, Anna, 72
Bormann, René, 30
Bourdieu, Pierre, 65
Bowie, David, 87
Brandstätter, Veronika, 39
Brickner, Irene, 116
Brown, Anna, 69
Butler, Judith, 34, 78, 79

C

Campbell, Naomi, 91
Carlson, Bronwyn, 18
Caron, Christina, 100
Carpenter, Dale, 43
Carter, David, 16, 53
Catania, Joseph A., 63
Chew-Bose, Durga, 87
Choi, Soon Kyo, 20, 25
Chong-suk, Han, 20
Clark, Andrew, 44
Clooney, George, 91
Cole, Shaun, 90
Colvin, Caroline, 68
Connell, R.W., 122
Connor, Christopher T., 104
Crookston, Cameron, 57

D

Daley, Tom, 37, 38
Diaz, Cameron, 91
Dib, Hiba, 23
Dietrich, Marlene, 87
Disney, Walt, 41, 44

Donahue, Rosemary, 127
Duberman, Martin, 16

E
Ecke, Matthias, 30, 31
Eco, Umberto, 90, 91
Emslie, Carol, 101
Eno, Brian, 87

F
Faiola, Anthony, 42
Fauck, Silvia, 42
Feinberg, Leslie, 13
Ferry, Bryan, 87, 88
Fischel, Joseph, 120
Flores, Buffy, 93
Foley, B. Fergus, 88
Forge, Nicholas, 49
Foucault, Michael, 78
Fredriksen-Goldsen, Karen I., 102
Frietsch, Ute, 70
Fritzsche, Bettina, 77

G
Garcia, Justin R., 45
Gernert, Johannes, 123
Giddens, Anthony, 73, 74
Gilbert, Sky, 108
Gössl, Martin J., 35, 41, 65, 76, 80, 94, 103, 112
Greenberg, Stefanie T., 124
Grinde, Bjorn, 125
Groh-Samberg, Olaf, 48
Gross, Larry, 35
Guzy, Lidia, 70

H
Hackmann, Kristina, 77
Halperin, David, 27, 34, 46, 54, 57, 70
Hanitzsch, Konstanze, 70
Harper, Gary, 13, 19
Hartmann, Jutta, 77
Hee, Amos, 20, 93
Henderson, Linda, 35
Hertel, Florian R., 48
Hilton-Morrow, Wendy, 98
Ho, Deborah, 24
Honneth, Axel, 33
Horn, Anita, 33
Hourani, Rad, 86, 87

I
Ireland, Lana, 101

J
Jagose, Anna-Marie, 71
James, Scott, 107
John, Jennifer, 27, 31, 70
Johnson, Marsha P., 16, 23

K
Kim, Hyun-Jun, 102
Kinsey, Alfred, 68
Klesse, Christian, 77

L
Lamot, Tom, 37
Langens, Thomas A., 39
Lau, Holning, 24
Lennox, Jemma, 101
Levine, Nick, 124

Lim, Gene, 18
Livingston, Jennie, 56

M
MacRae, Andrea Pauline, 89
Marcus, Eric, 13, 123
Mattson, Greggor, 59
McGee, Jordan, 89
Meyer, Ilan H., 133
Michaelis, Beatrice, 70
Ming Liu, William, 124
Minichiello, Victor, 93
Mitchell, Christopher, 58, 59
Moore, Chadwick, 114
Mulkerrins, Jane, 55

N
Naik, Yeshwant, 127
Nothing, Ehn, 14, 105

O
Otto, Jürgen H., 39

P
Paul, Jay, 63, 87
Peele, Thomas, 97
Petzold, Sebastian, 30, 31
Pew Research Center, 69
Plummer, Ken, 45
Pollack, Lance, 63
Pop, Iggy, 56, 87
Posch, Waltraud, 85, 86
Pyzyk, Katie, 60

R
Raab, Heike, 109
Rambo, 91
Ream, Geoffrey L., 49
Reed, 87
Reiber, Chris, 45
Ridge, Damien, 93
Ringer, Jeffrey, 35
Ritzer, George, 45
Rivera, Sylvia, 13–17, 20, 105
Robards, Brady, 18
Roberts, Julia, 91
Rodriguez-Jimenez, Jorge, 122
Roseneil, Sasha, 62
Rubin, Gayle S., 70, 73
RuPaul, 56, 57, 91, 108
Russell, Jamie, 84
Ryan, William S., 19, 133

S
Sánchez, Francisco J., 124
Schiffer, Claudia, 91
Sears, Brad, 24
Sedgwick, Eve Kosofsky, 114–116
Sigurdardóttir, Jóhanna, 40, 41
Sigusch, Volkmar, 128
Stall, Ron, 63
Staples, Louis, 61
Sturgis, Matthew, 32
Sutherland, Ruth, 40

T
Talusan, Meredith, 117
Thunderfuck, Alaska, 99
Traub, Valerie, 46
Tseng, Wei-Hong, 94

V

Vilain, Eric, 124

W

Wagenknecht, Peter, 77
Warner, Michael, 46, 47, 75, 79
Watson, Courtney, 68
Wicker, Randy, 15

Wilchins, Riki, 14, 15
Wilson, Bianca, 25
Winkler, Astrid, 121
Wong, Alia, 103
Woods, William J., 63

Y

Yiannopoulos, Milos, 114